What Curriculum
for the Information Age?

What Curriculum for the Information Age?

edited by

Mary Alice White
Teachers College, Columbia University

LAWRENCE ERLBAUM ASSOCIATES, PUBLISHERS
1987   Hillsdale, New Jersey   Hove and London

Lawrence Erlbaum Associates, Inc., Publishers
365 Broadway
Hillsdale, New Jersey 07642.

Library of Congress Cataloging-in-Publication Data

What curriculum for the information age?

   Includes bibliographies and index.
   1. Education—United States—Curricula.   2. Education
technology—United States—Curricula.   I. White, Mary
Alice.
LB1570.W48   1987   375'.00973   87-6741
ISBN 0-89859-922-0

Printed in the United States of America
10 9 8 7 6 5 4 3 2

Contents

5
CURRICULUM FOR THE INFORMATION AGE: AN INTERIM PROPOSAL
Julie McGee

6
GENERAL DISCUSSION

INDEX

Preface

This book has developed from a conference held at Teachers College, Columbia University on April 17, 1986, entitled "What Curriculum for the Information Age?" The conference was sponsored by the Electronic Learning Laboratory and the Department of Communication, Computing, and Technology in Education at Teachers College; the National School Boards Association, represented by James A. Mecklenburger, Director, Institute for the Transfer of Technology to Education; and the Corporation for Public Broadcasting, represented by Nancy Sceiford, Associate Director for Elementary and Secondary Educational Activities.

The idea for the conference evolved from discussions with the invited speakers who shared a concern that our public schools were not responding to the real potential that the information technologies hold for learning and for teaching. We felt that the educational issue was not what technologies to buy, where to put them, or when to schedule instruction on them.

We thought the real issue was the curriculum itself. Public schools needed to think very seriously about whether the present curriculum was adequate in the light of how the information technologies were changing access to information, the learning processes, and the very nature of information itself. It seemed to us that the time had come to change the focus of the school discussion from the notion that the technologies were an interesting adjunct to instruction, to the conception that the technologies represented a very basic change in what might be taught, and how it might be learned.

The contributors to this volume share quite different approaches to what that curriculum should be, ranging from recommending a basic change in what is taught, to a concern for the limitations of technology in teaching humanistic values. These differences in point of view are accentuated even more in the discussions at the end of each chapter. The discussions are led by four members of the faculty of Teachers College.

We did not seek unanimity. We did seek different, and clearly stated views of what a curriculum might be for the information age. It was our hope that such a debate might encourage similar discussions among educators, a curricular debate that we all agree is needed.

We extend appreciation to those who made the conference possible: John Fanselow, Robert McClintock, Roger Wyatt, and Betsy Currier of Teachers College; Jim Mecklenburger of the National School Boards Association; and Nancy Sceiford of CPB.

Mary Alice White

About the Contributors

Sam Gibbon is the producer of "The Voyage of the Mimi," a curricular project using the information technologies, designed for upper elementary grades in science and mathematics. He has been involved in several educational television projects, including "Sesame Street" and "1-2-3 Contact."

Julie McGee, formerly the director of educational software for Tandy's home marketing, is now associated with Ligature, publishing specialists in Chicago. She has been an experienced English teacher in public high school.

Diane Ravitch, author, critic, and lecturer, is Adjunct Professor of History and Education at Teachers College, Columbia University.

Judah L. Schwartz is Professor of Engineering Science and Education at Massachusetts Institute of Technology. He is also Co-Director of the Educational Technology Center and Professor of Education at Harvard University.

Mary Alice White is Director of the Electronic Learning Laboratory, and Professor of Psychology and Education, at Teachers College, Columbia University.

Learning and Instruction in the Information Age

Samuel Y. Gibbon, Jr.
Bank Street College of Education

The Information Age has arrived, and most societal institutions are experiencing profound changes as a result. Business, science, entertainment, medicine, communications and publishing, the law, banking, travel, government, the military, manufacturing, even agriculture have been or are being transformed by the presence of new electronic technologies, orchestrated by the computer and linked together over large and small distances. At a rate and to an extent envisioned only by the most extreme futurists the world is becoming interconnected by an electronic nervous system over which immense amounts of information flow at nearly the speed of light.

The lives of individuals and families are inevitably affected by these institutional transformations. For example, workers are finding that some familiarity with the new technologies of information is required in a large and increasing proportion of jobs. (Indeed, our economy is undergoing an accelerating transformation as the manufacture and distribution of information grows in importance.) But the impact of the Information Age is also felt directly in the home. Almost every home in the United States is connected to an efferent channel of the global electronic nervous system by means of a color television set. A slightly smaller number of homes is capable of two-way communication around the world by means of the telephone. In a small, but rapidly increasing number of homes, the telephone is being used to receive and transmit digital information from and to computers. And although the danger is yet to be fully recognized, the privacy of every citizen in our society is invaded regularly by organizations that use information technologies to compile dossiers of information for commercial or political purposes.

The power of the electronic technologies that drive the information explosion continues to increase rapidly, while at the same time their cost continues to fall dramatically. As a result, access to the means of generating and exchanging information, although still limited and subject to sharp demographic bias, has increased; and information now flows from a growing diversity of sources to an ever-increasing number of users.

Such widespread and important societal effects should be reflected in our educational agenda: Schools should prepare students to function successfully in a world continually transformed by new information. More importantly, the electronic information technologies should be used in schools, as they are elsewhere, to represent present knowledge in new ways and to make new knowledge.

Computerized electronic technology makes possible not only the wide and rapid distribution of information, but its manipulation, analysis, synthesis, and recombination as well. Through these operations, new knowledge is created that helps us understand ourselves and our world in new ways. Much of this new knowledge is, and will continue to be, expressed in printed language; but more and more is produced in other forms: images—still and moving, graphic and photographic; sounds—natural and synthesized; and non-alphanumeric symbolic representations of all kinds including icons, graphs, and geographic and conceptual maps. Some of these diverse forms, as well as the technology needed to produce them, have been invented in order to encode new meaning intelligibly. For example, Landsat images of the earth's surface made using electromagnetic wavelengths outside the visible spectrum must be "pseudo-colored" by computer in order to be "read" by the human eye and brain. Changes in surface vegetation can then be computed by subtracting one Landsat image from another and the result can be displayed in yet another pseudo-colored image. In other instances, the existence of new technological capabilities has stimulated the invention of new kinds of meaning. For example, graphic artists use computers to produce animated *trompes l'oeil* in which three-dimensional objects, complete with surface texture and reflected light, transform with mesmerizing impossibility into other shapes. As these examples suggest, the new technologies of information do more than increase the volume and speed of dissemination of information; they also extend the range of human senses, amplify the analytic power of the brain, and provide new instruments for creativity.

If these powerful technologies of the Information Age were as widely available in schools as they are in other societal organizations, what changes in curriculum content and in the paradigms of instruction would be indicated? Three overlapping categories of changes suggest themselves: additions to the curriculum, notably instruction about information itself and the technologies of information; changes in the content of the traditional curriculum; and changes in the structure of the curriculum and the style of classroom instruction.

ADDITIONS TO THE CURRICULUM

Information Studies

The principal addition to the curriculum called for by the arrival of the Information Age is a new emphasis on information itself. Students must learn to analyze critically its various forms and their characteristic uses, to recognize the ways in which opinion and behavior can be influenced by information, to search out needed information from the multiple sources available, to evaluate the quality of information, and to use the various media for effective communication. Reading, writing, critical analysis and evaluation of printed communications will continue to occupy a central position in the curriculum; but similar training must be provided in comprehending, analyzing, evaluating, and producing communications in visual media.

Students need to develop a repertoire of heuristics for judging the reliability of information. Some schools have undertaken to help students develop critical viewing skills with which to evaluate televised messages. Students in such programs acquire a useful skepticism about the claims of commercial advertisers and aspirants to political office and learn to look for evidence of bias in news reports. Students need to apply similar critical techniques to computer-based simulations or models. These can be powerful tools for analyzing and coming to understand complex systems or acquiring difficult skills in a risk-free environment; but students must learn to assess their veridicality. They must understand that the data and the operational rules that comprise the model or simulation are only selections from the complexity of the real world and that any model or simulation necessarily distorts, in discoverable ways, the system it represents.

A most useful way for students to learn this lesson is to construct a model themselves. Modeling a changing population for example can quickly lead to a vivid appreciation of the difficulty of model construction and the need for simplified assumptions. The electronic spreadsheet program is a tool for creating mathematical models of complex systems. It was created to allow the asking of "what if?" questions and the playing out of alternative financial scenarios, but it can be used to model other systems as well. Students should learn the power of this ubiquitous electronic tool by using it to construct and manipulate models.

Research Skills

Many careers in the information society will require skill in locating and retrieving information for which a need is known to exist. Even more valuable will be skill in combining information in novel ways so as to reveal an unsuspected opportunity or suggest a persuasive new point of view. In order to prepare young people for such careers, schools should offer students more frequent opportunities to pursue their own education through self-directed scholarship, guided and overseen by teachers, but not overly constrained as to subject matter. To this end, research skills taught to graduate students 20 years ago and to undergraduates 10 years ago should now be a routine part of the high-school curriculum. These should include, in addition to the library skills familiar to generations of book scholars, techniques for searching the on-line and off-line databases now available in large libraries. By teaching students to navigate a hierarchical tree of information or to search by multiple key words or to use Boolean statements to define the search domain, teachers can lead students to an understanding of the several ways in which knowledge can be organized; and this in turn can help students choose appropriate organizing structures for their own bodies of information.

As in the case of models, a most effective way for students to learn how to negotiate an electronic knowledge base is to create one of their own. Here, an opportunity exists to anticipate in the classroom a category of work that is just beginning to establish itself in the information society: community authorship. Classroom-wide research projects are, of course, not new; but electronic tools can facilitate collaboration of a kind and to an extent not previously possible. Local area networks with integrated word-processing and database management software allow students to work together in editing, amplifying, annotating, and organizing in multiple ways information they have retrieved from existing sources or generated themselves. For many students, collaborative creation of this kind can liberate talents whose exercise may have been inhibited by more traditional, and more competitive, individual authorship.

Typing

True voice-recognition technology at affordable cost remains in the distant future, so the alphanumeric keyboard will continue to be the principle device by means of which information in the form of language is generated, retrieved, and communicated. Word processing, network access, and electronic mail require use of the typewriter keyboard. In order to enjoy full enfranchisement in the Information Age, all students need to learn touch typing. (The author, whose education was deficient in this respect, feels this need most poignantly at the present moment.) The professional status of typing has changed rapidly and dramatically since the arrival of the computer in the workplace. Formerly, typing was the domain of the clerical worker, usually female, and typing classes were offered as vocational training in high school. If a young woman wished to be taken seriously as a professional she was often advised not to learn to type, lest she find herself trapped by her competence at a clerical level. In the last 10 years, the computer terminal, with its typewriter keyboard, has come to be as common a sight in executive offices as it is on the secretarial desks outside, and the gender of the respective users is beginning to be less predictable.

CHANGES IN THE TRADITIONAL CURRICULUM

Reading and Writing

The huge and growing volume of printed information requires the development of reading skills in addition to those traditionally taught in elementary school. Students must be taught to browse efficiently in various media, but especially in text. Attention to indices, menus, section headings, topic sentences and summaries, visual scans for key words, skimming, and other browsing skills need to be explicitly taught, and taught early, in part because of the emphasis in early reading on word-for-word, beginning-to-end reading. Instruction in reading comprehension presently addresses some of these skills, but the main emphasis in pre-college reading instruction is on fine analysis of grammatical and syntactic subtleties. Students also need to learn to discriminate those tasks and passages that merit close, careful reading from those for which fast scanning and breadth of survey are more appropriate.

To the varieties of reading matter students presently encounter in schools should be added screen plays and television scripts. Exposure to scripts will help children understand the structure and techniques of the visual media to which they frequently attend without thought. It can be enlightening to discover that the casually delivered, fragmentary utterances of television or film drama have actually been written, and that the sequence of visual images has been conceived with care to convey meaning. An examination of the written transcript of a television documentary can often reveal the purpose for which a particular juxtaposition of word and image was contrived. Television scripts and film screenplays have high intrinsic interest for the otherwise unmotivated reader, and some such documents even have literary merit.

Similarly, children should be encouraged to write many different kinds of texts. A language arts class might be assigned to write the following different treatments of a recent actual event: a journalistic account for a daily newspaper, an analytic piece for a weekly news magazine, a report from a remote location for the nightly television news, and fictionalized accounts in the form of a short story and in the form of a screenplay. Writing these various assignments would make clear the extent to which the purpose of the writer, the characteristics of the medium, and the demands of the marketplace condition the character of the message; it would encourage critical consumption of similar accounts in the mass media; and it would develop an awareness of the skills necessary for professional performance of the work.

Every student should learn to write using a word processor, and schools should make microcomputer-based word processing easily available to all students during and outside of regular school hours. The principles of good composition are readily taught and willingly practiced when text can be edited without effort. At present, research and development are being vigorously pursued to discover how computer-based writing environments with some artificial intelligence can be designed to support the efforts of the student writer. Writing instruction is one area of the curriculum in which schools are likely to keep abreast of new technological developments.

In schools properly equipped for the Information Age, of course, the writing assignments just described would be carried through to production and publication. Formatting software, graphics packages, and sophisticated printers allow the publication of documents that look as if they had been professionally printed. In the process of producing such documents, students can explore the effect of variations in such important design features as type size and font selection, column width and column breaks, page layout, graphic style, and balance between text and graphics.

The video writing assignments should be produced as well. Here, the design elements include sets, costumes, props, lighting, illustrative graphics, and so on. But the most valuable lessons will be learned in editing the resulting images. Students can then discover how profoundly and undetectably the meaning of a sequence can be altered by such techniques as cutting or reordering what someone says, inserting a reaction shot, adding music to the sound track, or choosing to make a transition with a dissolve instead of a cut.

The purpose of these production and publishing experiences is not merely to inoculate students against manipulation by the media. It is to make students literate in the communications of their culture, so they can appreciate skillful use of the media by others and can themselves communicate effectively.

Mathematics

Electronic technology has occasioned a re-examination of the mathematics curriculum. Clearly, the ubiquity of electronic calculators has made it less necessary the ability to perform with pencil and paper such tedious large calculations as long division and adding long columns of multi-digit numbers. It seems appropriate for students to understand the principles behind such arithmetic operations but not appropriate for them to spend long hours of drill perfecting the execution of the algorithms in repetitive problem sets.

If classroom time devoted to training in calculation can be reduced, then more time will be available for more important mathematics (e.g., problem analysis, estimation, rounding, approximation, place value, and orders of magnitude). The availability of calculators has made these skills and concepts more, rather than less, necessary. Students tend to have excessive confidence in results arrived at electronically, even if the answer displayed by the calculator is highly unlikely. This misplaced confidence must be reduced, and students must develop the habit of checking their computed answers for reasonability by performing quick rough mental calculations.

Learning a few tricks of arithmetic can make these rough calculations easier. For example, adding or subtracting from left to right gives a rough approximation at once. The procedure can be continued until the result is as precise as the situation requires. Using the conventional algorithm (adding or subtracting from right to left) gives the least useful information first: the units place of a six-digit sum is less informative about the magnitude of the number than the hundred thousands place. Tricks involving recombining numbers are useful. For example, multiplying by 50 is easier if you divide by 2 and add two zeros to the result. These and other familiar tricks of mental arithmetic develop a feeling for the structure of the number system. They give students a sense of intellectual power and confidence that the calculator technology is under their control.

Electronic technology can provide a rich variety of powerful mathematics learning experiences. Interactive computer graphics can be used to present mathematical relations in visually concrete form, manipulable by the student. Geometric relations are particularly amenable to such presentation. For example, the properties of a right triangle can be explored by manipulating the lengths of the legs, changing the sizes of the acute angles but always maintaining their sum at $90°$. The Pythagorean relation can be similarly explored. Squares drawn on each side of the right triangle can grow and shrink as the length of the legs are changed, while the relation among the squares can be seen to remain constant. Two aspects of such presentations are essential: The transformations must be as smoothly continuous as possible and they must be under the direct and instantaneous control of the student. When these two conditions are met, explorations of this kind can provide a visual/kinesthetic understanding of mathematical principles. Later, when abstract formulations of the principles are introduced, they can be understood with reference to the earlier concrete experience.

Electronic technologies in combination can embed math concepts and problems in highly motivating "real-world" contexts. A dramatic television segment can set the problem, show engaging characters struggling to solve it, perhaps under considerable dramatic pressure, and then play out the solution as the dramatic conflict is resolved. Microcomputer software can then present analogous problems for the student to solve. "The Voyage of the Mimi," a federally funded science and math project that combines video segments, microcomputer software and text material, uses this technique repeatedly. For example, in one episode the captain of the sailing vessel Mimi sets a course toward a dangerous shoal. An electrical problem causes his knotmeter (a nautical speedometer) to malfunction. The captain measures Mimi's speed by timing the boat's passage past a piece of bread thrown in the water. The calculation confirms the captain's suspicions: The boat has been traveling faster than the indicated speed and therefore has gone farther toward the shoals than the captain had intended. He must now quickly determine the boat's actual position. He triangulates Mimi's location by taking two compass bearings with the boat's radio direction finder; where the bearings cross, there lies Mimi, perilously close to the rocks. Students who watch this episode in class are absorbed by the dramatic action. Because the mathematics of navigation is central to the resolution of the problem, they remember most of the details; and they are motivated to address the next task: using computer-simulated instruments to solve an analogous navigation problem. The math concepts are difficult, but the dramatic demonstration of their value in a life-threatening situation sustains students' interest through the hard work.

Perhaps the greatest need in math education is for the development of mathematical good sense. Mathematical statements abound in the Information Age: estimates of risk, projections of deficits, population growth curves, and measurements in gigawatts, femtoseconds, light years, and megatons. Too often the statements are accepted without examination, the numbers simply ignored. The words "billion" and "million" sound so much alike that they are often confused; but because the magnitudes referred to are so poorly comprehended, the confusion goes unnoticed. At the same time, statements containing numbers, especially large ones, are assumed to be authoritative, whether or not they are understood. Charlatans of every stripe can confidently count on the innumeracy of the public. Schools must help students become detectors of mathematical nonsense.

Science

Post-secondary science education, like science itself, is being transformed by the power of electronic technology. Elementary science education, on the other hand, is only beginning to take advantage of the new learning tools available to it. Three classes of computer applications deserve wider use: computer-based laboratory instruments, simulations of natural phenomena not otherwise easily observed, and dynamic models of complex systems. These computer tools can facilitate hands-on experimental observation and measurement, enlarge the range of student experiences, and introduce at an elementary level a powerful analytic tool of science.

Microcomputer-based laboratories (MBLs) use the microcomputer to collect, display, and analyze laboratory data. Sensors have been developed to measure a wide variety of phenomena including temperature, light intensity, sound amplitude and frequency, acidity, and electrical resistance. The analog information collected by the sensors is converted to digital form and stored as data in the computer's memory, whence it can be recalled for display in numerical form or in graphs of various kinds. Mathematical manipulations can be performed on the stored data and the results of these analyses can themselves be displayed in different forms.

The advantages of computer-based instrumentation are several. First, elementary-school laboratories have generally not included equipment to measure such a diversity of phenomena; the cost and management problems have been too great. The MBL makes these measurements convenient and inexpensive. As a result, students can acquire hands-on laboratory experiences they could not have enjoyed previously. Because the equipment is easy to use, students "mess about" enthusiastically, discovering both the properties of the phenomenon they are measuring and the characteristics of the measurement device. These initial explorations give rise to questions that lead naturally and spontaneously to informal experiments.

Second, a distinctive feature of computerized instruments is that their measurement scales are not fixed. For example, the range of an MBL thermometer scale can be set by the experimenter to reflect the range of temperatures expected in the experiment. If the cooling to room temperature of a beaker of boiling water is to be measured, the scale can be set to measure from $100°$ C to $20°$ C. If variations in body temperature are to be measured the scale can be set to display a much narrower range, say $35°$ C to $40°$ C. Students quickly come to appreciate the value of choosing a scale of measurement that provides data of appropriate resolution.

Third, MBL measurements can be taken continuously over time and the results displayed as a two-dimensional graph. Like the measurement scale, the time scale of the graph can be set by the experimenter and can range from a few seconds to several days. Because the measurements are taken and the graph is drawn continuously as the experiment proceeds, the graph is easily understood to be a mathematical "picture" of an event. Furthermore, a little experience with the graphing function gives students an intuitive understanding of the slope of the graph. The data analysis and graphing capability of the MBL integrates mathematics into the science curriculum easily and naturally.

Finally, MBL sensors require regular calibration, an apparent inconvenience that can be turned to instructional advantage. The need for calibration impresses upon students the fact that all measurement devices have built-in error. Students confront at once a central fact of experimental science. The value of careful calibration, accurate record-keeping, replication, and examination of data for systematic error are quickly evident.

The cumulative effect of these several advantages of the microcomputer-based laboratory is that students in elementary-science classes can be acting and therefore thinking like scientists from the beginning. It is important to recognize that MBL experiments are not simulations; they are genuine hands-on laboratory activities conducted with instrumentation that offers special advantages for learning.

Microcomputer simulations can play an important role in science instruction. When an activity is too dangerous or too complicated to be managed in a school laboratory, or when ideal rather than actual worlds are to be explored, the simulation can be most useful. For example, controlling the motion of a simulated space ship by firing its rocket thrusters or bouncing a simulated billiard ball around a table with adjustable friction can provide an experiential foundation on which theoretical understanding can subsequently be built.

The third computer application, dynamic modeling of complex systems, can both help students understand the complicated interactions among factors in the modeled systems and sensitize students to the caution that must be exercised in drawing conclusions about the actual system from the behavior of the model. Students can change the values assigned to the parameters that comprise the model and observe the consequences. For example, a model of a closed ecosystem allows students to select a limited number of plants, animals, and pond organisms to comprise a food chain, then select an initial population level for each organism and observe what happens to the population balance over the course of several years. Varying the predator–prey relationships and the initial population densities produces widely divergent outcomes. A more sophisticated model would permit varying other parameters: birth and death rates, for example, or nutritional needs, or climate.

Many highly sophisticated computer models exist in university science laboratories. As microcomputers get more powerful, some of these models may be adapted for use in elementary and secondary classrooms. For example, a minicomputer model of a DNA molecule allows the scientist, and student, to rotate the molecule or travel through it, exploring its helical structure. Astronomers have modeled the beautiful and dramatic tidal effects produced by the close encounter of two galaxies. A young student would not understand these models as a graduate student might understand them, but the striking images would be added to the student's experiential repertoire to be understood better, or differently, later on.

The full implications for the science curriculum of the availability of these advanced technologies are not yet entirely clear. It does appear that computers make possible some kinds of scientific explorations that were previously impossible or available only to more advanced students. Careful research is needed to discover the developmental suitability of these activities for young students.

Television has had a significant impact on the scientific understanding of young students. A child of school age today has probably been exposed to more images of the natural and man-made worlds than could have been seen in the span of an entire lifetime at any previous period in human history. This huge library of images constitutes a resource that can be drawn upon in the child's education. On the other hand, many of the images stored in the child's mind are distorted, either through the deliberate action of the maker of the image or through the imperfect understanding of the viewing child. Furthermore, some of the most distorted images are those of science, scientists, and scientific subject matter. Schools should make extensive use of the many films and television programs that accurately depict the world and the scientists who discover its structures. Children learn effortlessly and with pleasure from these programs, and teachers can use them not only to correct the distorted views their students may have acquired from other less reliable sources but to help students become discriminating consumers of televised information.

Social Studies

Many of the same techniques of modeling and simulation that have proved useful in science education can enrich the social studies curriculum as well. Computer-based adventure games simulate the experience of travelling west on the Oregon Trail or conducting the battle of Waterloo. Some simulation games have been designed to be played simultaneously by entire classrooms of students. These simulations help students learn about the economics of manufacturing, the discovery and exploration of the new world, or the pressures affecting negotiations between nations. Teachers and students who have used these simulations have found them engrossing and convincing. For this very reason, students should be encouraged to consider in what respects the simulations accurately reflect the events or processes simulated and in what respects they do not. Because the computer programs are highly appealing, students may be motivated to search other sources for confirming or amplifying information.

Computer-accessed databases are valuable sources of information for these and other student researches. Database management software can help students organize the information they acquire. This most useful software tool has been less widely used than its more familiar companion programs, the word processor and the electronic spreadsheet, perhaps because the type of investigation it supports has not been generally recognized as a coherent intellectual activity of value in many domains.

At present, most databases reside in mainframe computers that must be accessed by telephone line. Charges are assessed depending on the duration of connect time, and they can be steep. An alternative technology for storing large databases is the compact disc (CD), the same laser-read medium that now delivers noise-free digital sound to stereo systems. Compact discs can be used to store very large databases consisting of digitally encoded text and images as well as sound. The Library of Congress is in the process of encoding some 4 million machine-readable catalogue files on a compact disc. It is likely that early in the next century much of the actual contents of the Library will be available on video disc or on CD. Indexing systems now being developed will employ artificial intelligence to assist the researcher in defining the research task and in finding the relevant material.

Among the public resources appropriate for distribution on videodisc and CD are the immense visual archives of NASA, NOAA, and the National Weather Service. The astonishing images these agencies have provided of our Earth and the other planets of the solar system are available to revitalize an important part of the social studies curriculum. Geography has reclaimed our attention as we have learned just how fragile and threatened are our shared earthly resources, how remarkable are our companion planets, and how unique Earth is among them.

It seems fitting that social studies in the Information Age should take advantage of telecommunications networks that can put people in touch with one another across political and cultural boundaries. Computer networks make possible direct on-line communication between individuals or non-synchronous communications among the members of a group sharing common interests. International electronic communities of adults have flourished for some years. An international educational telecommunications network could link class-rooms of children around the world for the purpose of exchanging information and opinions on matters of mutual concern. Communications might touch on such topics as differences and similarities of lifestyle and culture, political issues and sports, and might ultimately include a wide variety of personal messages between new friends. Such a "Worldnet" might begin by linking nodes located at a few science and technology centers around the world. From there the network connections could proliferate.

Music and Art

Computer-based electronic tools are changing the practice of the creative arts. Many of these tools require only a microcomputer; all, including those that call for special equipment, are becoming more powerful and less expensive. Elementary- and secondary-school teaching in the creative arts should take advantage of these empowering tools, and curricula should be revised to reflect the changes in the arts brought about by their use.

The music synthesizer has made it possible for a musician to "play" an entire orchestra and to invent new musical sounds of limitless variety. Music-editing software has done for music writing, orchestration, and scoring what the word processor has done for the production of text. For students of all levels of skill, the new music hardware and software makes the study of both theory and practice more accessible. Music instruction should no longer be the prov-ince of the talented few; all students should have the opportunity to learn the rudiments of musical form and notation. Beginning students can learn the conventions of musical notation by listening and watching as a computer plays a simple composition and simultaneously displays its printed score with a moving highlight. Ear-training software can help students learn to recognize acoustically presented musical intervals and to associate them with their written equivalents. Students of harmony who are unable to play a keyboard instrument can now hear their composition exercises performed by the computer on which they were written, and then revise them. Instrumental students can practice performing with a computer-generated orchestra that is tireless, inexpensive, easily scheduled, dynamically controllable, and, if audited with headphones, unheard by others.

The electronic synthesizer allows the musician to construct a musical tone by adding frequencies to a basic wave form to alter the timbre of the sound. The attack and decay of the tone can be adjusted as well. Consequently, a sophisticated synthesizer can be made to sound remarkably like any conventional instrument or to produce sounds that can be made in no other way. Because all the components of the sound can be displayed graphically and controlled, the physics of musical sound is more evident and available for instructional exploitation than ever before, and a collaboration between the science teacher and the music teacher is feasible.

Critical study of the visual arts stands to benefit from information technology. Laser videodiscs containing visual databases make it possible for the student of art history to examine the entire oeuvre of an artist, or for that matter of an entire school of artists. The search speed of the videodisc player makes it possible to compare sequentially any 2 of the 54,000 images stored on a single side of a video disc within a second or two. Videodisc technology also facilitates the study of film and video. Sequences can be played through frame by frame to examine editing techniques, to analyze special effect photography, or to discover lapses in continuity.

Computers constitute a new medium of artistic expression with which images are produced that differ in character from those produced using other media. "Paint" software places at the disposal of the computer artist palettes with colors numbering in the tens of thousands, electronic "brushes" that can themselves be designed by the artist, geometric tools for drawing shapes of all kinds, and a scale-change function that enlarges a section of the image for detail work and then reduces it to its former size. Still more elaborate design software allows an artist to construct an image by a combination of drawing and computation. Such images may include three-dimensional objects that are opaque or transparent, lit by cast light from any direction chosen by the artist, with surface texture ranging from smooth to fuzzy. These images can be transformed mathematically. If each frame of transformation is filmed or recorded, and the sequence of frames played back at projection speed, remarkable animation effects can be produced.

At present, the hardware and software necessary to make such images is sufficiently expensive to restrict its use to computer graphic professionals; but slightly less powerful microcomputer versions of these design tools are available now at prices schools can afford, and new generations of micros will within a few years put the capability of today's professional technology at the disposal of elementary school students.

Similarly, electronic enhancement and editing of photographs, today a common technique in magazine publishing, is likely, given the inexorable downward trend of costs, to be available soon to the student photographer. Low-cost computerized video editing equipment, including digital frame storage and digital image processing, is in development for use with $1/2$ in. or 8mm video tape. The tools of the video artist will then be available not only to professionals but to students as well.

A most significant feature of computer-based artistic productions is that they can consist of combinations of media. Text, graphics, moving images, and synthesized sound can be woven together into a single presentation. Such works are developed by groups of artists collaborating together or by individual artists working alone. Computers are enabling the development of multi-talented electronic artists, the equipment is more readily available, and galleries and museums are beginning to exhibit the work.

The art curriculum in elementary and secondary schools should be expanded to include an introduction to electronic art. This is important for two reasons: First, students should be given some familiarity with the various artistic media of their culture; and second, electronic images are used more and more in the Information Age, and visual literacy must be grounded in an understanding of how the images are produced. But the school art curriculum should not abandon the traditional media of the visual arts. The eye is informed by the hand, and the development of a student's visual sensibilities is well served by learning to represent what is seen with materials that are directly tactile.

CHANGES IN STRUCTURE AND STYLE

In the previous section, discussion of changes in the school curriculum was organized according to traditional curriculum domains. Here a broader, structural change is proposed: For some substantial fraction of the late elementary- and secondary-school schedule the boundaries between curriculum domains should be blurred deliberately, and the perspectives of several disciplines should be brought to bear on a single complex real-world topic.

In early elementary school, students are customarily in the charge of a single classroom teacher who controls, for better or worse, their intellectual fortunes for the entire school year. Specialists in reading, science, or math may pay an occasional visit, but for the most part, education is delivered by a single person. That person may arrange the instruction in clearly separated units on reading, social studies, arithmetic, and so on, but cross-referencing among the units is not only possible, it is likely, given the continuity of teacher and learning population. Moreover, the teacher serves as a continuously available model of integrated learning.

Sometime around the transition from elementary to secondary school the increasing complexity of subject matter requires that instruction be delivered entirely by specialists. The effect is to unravel the weave of knowledge, leaving only the warp. The long threads of science, history, literature, mathematics, art, and the rest lie alongside one another, unconnected; the integrating weft, necessary to hold the fabric together, is not supplied. The only commonalities evident across subject matters are administrative: class length, class size, the hierarchical arrangement of furniture, the inevitability of tests. Nevertheless, we expect that the learner, uninstructed in the art of integrating knowledge, with neither human nor institutional models to emulate, will somehow contrive to weave together the separate strands of the curriculum and become an educated person. This is, it seems to me, an unreasonable expectation.

There is no escaping the necessity of specialized teaching. It arises from the increasing specialization of knowledge in the world outside schools. Indeed, as the generation of new knowledge in the Information Age approaches the pace of explosion, specialties tend to subdivide into ever narrower domains of expertise. Yet, at the same time, the electronic technologies of information have helped us understand as never before the complexity and interconnectedness of natural and manmade systems, and the startling variety of effects that can cascade from a single cause. We have learned that many bodies of expert knowledge, narrow in scope, must be assembled into larger structures of understanding if we are to survive our global problems and exploit our opportunities. And if our schools are to prepare young people to contribute to these larger systems of knowledge, then the curriculum must include not only the specialized instruction that is presently offered but regular, developmentally appropriate opportunities for integrated, collaborative, multi-disciplinary study as well.

Topic-driven multi-disciplinary learning opportunities enjoy a number of advantages. First, each disciplinary perspective is validated by its relevance to the topic under study; school subjects can be seen to have value in clarifying issues that matter to students. Second, an individual student may choose from among the analytic, synthetic, expressive, and problem-solving tools of the several curriculum domains those that seem most useful or congenial; but the community of students will exercise them all, and the complementary value of the different intellectual approaches will be evident to all the participants. Third, complex real-world topics are likely to arouse emotions, stimulate imagination, and provoke sharp differences of opinion; this makes the learning more compelling for the student and the teaching more satisfying for the teacher.

Multi-disciplinary study can of course, be conducted successfully using resources no more exotic than the school library, the art room, the science lab, and an appropriate field trip or two, and even the most electronically well-endowed school will make full use of these traditional resources. But where they are available, the electronic technologies of the Information Age can enrich multi-disciplinary learning in several ways.

First, study topics can be given vivid presentation. Television in particular can offer powerful vicarious experience of people, places, and subjects otherwise inaccessible to students. Second, the ramifications of the topic can be explored through the use of computer databases, videodisc and compact disc archives, computer-based expert systems, telecommunications networks and computer analytic tools. Finally, the results of the study can be presented to interested others by a combination of reporting media including: articles written, illustrated, composed, and printed using computers; video documents composed of footage assembled and edited from archival material or produced on tape by students; audio reports, including, for example, long-distance telephone interviews with experts; and computer analyses generated by students, using existing software or programs written especially for the purpose. Planning and executing these multi-media reports can be pedagogically useful in several ways: (a) the student authors will increase their mastery of the subject matter, (b) other students will be inclined to attend to the instruction of their peers, and (c) the authors will increase their understanding of the several media used.

Most significantly, electronic technologies now make possible direct interactive access by the learner to simultaneous (non-sequential) representations of complex systems. The result can be learning which is mediated not exclusively by language, but by visual, auditory, and kinesthetic experience as well.

The motivational and intellectual advantages of integrating study across disciplines accrue to all subjects, but they have a particular value for science and mathematics, two areas of the curriculum that many students find bloodless and alienating and from which, therefore, they are inclined to retire. For example, "The Voyage of the Mimi," the multi-media science and math project referred to earlier, treats a topic that is universally interesting and a likely candidate for cross-disciplinary study but that is not easily available for firsthand study: the great whales. Concentrating on whales can nicely serve the needs of the science curriculum because whales can be considered not only as biological organisms that reproduce and metabolize but also as physical entities that produce sound waves, radiate heat, and undergo large pressure changes, as collections of chemical reactions including those caused by the polluting effluents of human activity, as intelligent beings whose cognition and communication are highly complex, and so on. The mathematics curriculum is encountered at many junctures, because each scientific investigation needs to be quantitatively based and requires a variety of calculations. Whales themselves are interesting objects to measure and count, and the difficulty of both activities can require mathematical ingenuity.

Although science and mathematics are the main curriculum concerns of "The Voyage of the Mimi," teachers have found fruitful connections to other curriculum domains as well. Whales have been the subject of literature, song, art, and myth; students can both appreciate the work of other artists and execute artistic compositions of their own. The commercial exploitation of whales played an important role in the economic history of the new world. For similar reasons they are today the subject of acrimonious negotiations among governments. Some non-trivial conflicts of values are involved. For example, several Eskimo groups rely for their food supply on annual harvests of whales. Some whale researchers present evidence that the whale pods preyed upon are endangered by the practice and have demanded that traditional whaling be banned along with the mechanized slaughter carried out by a few industrial nations. Eskimos argue that they have been dependent on whales for thousands of years, that they know more about the whale populations on which they depend than the scientists from the South, and that their traditional way of life is threatened by the proposed ban. What should the International Whaling Commission do?

Students and teachers might take on the roles of the commissioners and the contending parties, develop and weigh the evidence in support of the positions, examine the commission's charter to determine what actions it can take, consider the effects on relations among the member states of each course of action, and finally debate the limits, if any, that ethical considerations impose on the predatory behavior of the animal at the top of the food chain.

Collaborative multi-disciplinary studies can have significant effects on the politics of the classroom and on the style of classroom interaction. It will be advantageous for several teachers to work together in preparing and carrying out the work. This will ensure that the various curriculum disciplines are responsibly represented, and it will give students an opportunity to observe and emulate adult models of cooperation and mutual support. Ultimately, however, responsibility for deciding on the work to be done must be shared among all the learners, students and teachers alike. This will require adjustments on both sides. Students are no more accustomed than teachers to collaborating in decisions about what is to be learned. The sharing of responsibility will be salubrious for both groups. Students can have a strong feeling of shared achievement and of shared ownership of the results of their work. The relation between student and teacher can begin to transform into the relation of apprentice to master, where the skill to be learned is knowing how to learn.

A well-chosen topic of study will extend beyond the limits of expertise of each of the teachers who collaborates in administering it. This will provide an opportunity for every teacher to say truthfully, "I don't know; but that's a great question. How do you think you can find out?" It is not easy for teachers to place themselves deliberately in a situation where their command of the content to be learned is less than masterful. However, it can be liberating for their students; from the ensuing experience students can begin to learn to conceive of themselves as capable of independent learning and to develop an appetite for lifelong learning. The role of the teacher is no less important under these altered circumstances than it was when the teacher was the source of all knowledge. Now the teacher is guide, mentor, coach, example, and counselor.

One centrally important function the teacher must perform in collaborative multi-disciplinary studies is to help students deal with their emotions. Learning experiences of this sort are liable to generate strong feelings, some of them in response to the collaborative situation itself, but some also in response to the information that the group develops. The fears, hurts, jealousies, and joys that come from working closely together need to be shared and discussed openly, so that students can learn the skills of collaboration. Less familiar to teachers may be the strength of the emotions aroused in their students by the information the group acquires.

Much conventional classroom instruction deals in information that is remarkably bland. Textbook publishers strive to avoid any hint of controversy. Instruction in conventional subject areas tends to be unconnected with the real life of the student, and therefore free of emotional entailment. But in the attentional economy of the child, that information is worth attending to which evokes an emotional response or triggers a flight of the imagination or both; so schools find ways of stimulating student feelings in order that curriculum information will be attended to. Desire for approval and apprehension of failure are the two emotions to which schools most frequently resort. When students and teachers embark on collaborative, topic-driven multi-disciplinary studies, however, they re-enter the real world. Students may find themselves confronting information that is disturbing, upsetting of their previous beliefs, angering, moving, giddily exciting. Teachers must help students master their emotions by expressing them. The purpose, of course, is not to sanitize the information; the emotion felt is part of the knowing. But children often need help, first to avoid being overwhelmed by the emotions they feel, and then to evaluate critically the information that aroused the strong feelings.

From multi-disciplinary study students learn the interconnectedness of things. More important, they learn to look for interconnections. Seymour Papert has quoted Gregory Bateson to the effect that each act of learning becomes a model for learning itself. If a student is repeatedly exposed to discontinuous learning experiences, then for that student learning comes to be characterized by discontinuity. If, by contrast, the student experiences integrated learning then integrated learning is what the student subsequently seeks. Schools have an obligation to provide models of integrated learning.

Finally, I believe schools must help students think epistemologically. The study of information suggested earlier as an addition to the curriculum can begin the process. Critical analysis of messages delivered using the media of the

Information Age, development of heuristics for evaluating information, studying the abuse of the information technologies, these activities can lead the student to consider such issues as how perception operates, the role of feedback mechanisms in human and machine intelligence, the significance of self-reference, the ways in which computers and human brains are alike and different. The progress toward epistemological self-awareness can be advanced in the course of the multi-disciplinary investigations just proposed. For example, as students discover common patterns across the boundaries of traditional curriculum disciplines, they can become self-consciously aware of the pattern-seeking character of human intelligence. The ultimate aim is to induce students to ponder such fundamental epistemological questions as why we believe what we believe, what constitutes credible evidence, and what is the nature of knowing. No more useful preparation can be provided for life in the Information Age.

DISCUSSION

Professor Hazel Hertzberg,
Teachers College (Social Studies)

I am going to attack this—probably somewhat more strongly than is justified, but I think that we need some countervailing views to this brave new world of the computer. I am going to start with Dewey's definition of *education*, which is that education is the reorganization or the reconstruction of experience. Think of the computer, television, or any other such mechanical tool in terms of how it may detract from or enrich that process between the learner and what he or she is learning. The person should be able to reconstruct that experience within him or herself if education is going to take. I am very concerned about the effect of a computer on this process.

Let me make a few comments on what Sam Gibbon has said. First of all, watch the language. We really should be able (I hope, if the computer has the humanistic possibilities that are claimed for it) to talk about it in another language. I do not think that it is wise to cast the student as a *consumer,* or the teacher as a *manager* of experience, or technology as *teacher-intensive,* or interchange in the classroom as *feedback* or *input.* These are mechanical terms drawn largely from the vocabulary of scientific management and they inevitably shape how we think. I would also caution the reader to ask what the real world is. We have had many references to the real world and assumptions that the real world will appear on the computer in a more refined technology. Any such object selects carefully in terms of its own possibilities and the person who is doing the selection what you see of the real world is not the real world out there. That is not concrete experience. It is experience at second hand, just the way the book is experience at second hand, although I think it requires less imagination. So I think we ought to examine the language in which we discuss this problem.

Secondly, let us look at the impact of television on schools. It seems to me that the impact of television has been very profound, but schools did not rise to the occasion. I was a teacher in a junior high school when television came into education with some real force. The school bought some sets but nobody used them. Television has not had, at least in the field of social studies, many important uses in the classroom. What has happened, however, is that people have been profoundly affected—the whole society, the politics of the society, the way we perceive life. The tremendous confusions over time and space exist in our society, or in any society in which television is so important. These confusions have not been discussed in the classroom. They have not been subject to scrutiny. I think the field of social studies has been very remiss in that. Students should study the history of technology and its impact, and what it has done to the quality of life of human beings, which will obviously be seen to improve in some ways and not in others. They will then be able to trace some development in the use of technology so they will be better prepared for the new technology that will inevitably come in our lifetimes and certainly in theirs. I notice that nothing was said about history in these curricular recommendations, and perhaps it was an oversight, but I believe that history is the most difficult subject, and the social studies much more difficult I suspect, to put on a computer. I have never seen a good program, although I think geography might be a candidate for one, and I think good programs are possible.

What I am suggesting in part is that the classroom itself is perhaps a relic of an older time in society. I am talking about the self-contained classroom in which the teacher is the artisan and the students are apprentices working along with the teacher. That is a very valuable model. The reason why they have held on to that way of approaching knowledge is because the classroom is a counterbalancing force to many other forces in society, and in the classroom the teacher has some control.

I believe the school has to be a countervailing force. The school cannot just accept computers uncritically. Nor can it accept computers critically without looking at the very basis of the claims for computers itself, including the claims of very articulate and humane people who do not wish them to be accepted uncritically.

In terms of the curriculum in my own field the most important thing to do is to consider this problem historically, in terms of the development of technology, and of change through time. Computers will obviously be replaced, or superceded, or added to, by some other such technology in the next 20 or 30 years. If you have an historical perspective, you know that change is inevitable and that change in this direction is probably going to happen. I do not want to see us come out of this information-rich but wisdom-poor. I believe that the most important things that one has to learn from the human past have to do in the end with wisdom, not with simply information.

One comment about team teaching. I am all for it, I have seen it work well in some places and not so well in others. Although the computer may force team teaching, in some fields, I do not believe that is going to affect the social studies field. Often, the problem with team teaching is that there is no conceptual base for it. You have an English teacher teaching English, a social studies teacher teaching history, and never the twain shall meet. There has to be a genuine integration of some sort to make this successful, to make it possible for students to reconstruct their experience rather than just be consumers. I do not see that integration happening by way of the computer. That is something that has to be thought about very carefully away from a computer.

I suspect that most of the books that I hope will continue to be produced for our students to read will be written on computer. I write books on a computer myself. I like the word processor. But I do not see in my field that the computer will play the kind of role that has been mentioned. The most important thing in my field is to examine this phenomenon historically and critically.

I close by saying something quite reactionary. The assumption is made that the people who have access to a computer are somehow richer than the people who do not. That may well be true in terms of access to certain kinds of power. I am not convinced that the societies that are rich in computers will be richer in wisdom than those societies that are not, any more than I see that our society is richer for television. In fact, I would maintain that with all the benefits of television and I see many, there are ways in which television creates heroes for our children, creates a spurious image often of reality, has very confused moral messages, and has certainly, as any high-school teacher will tell you, greatly cut down on reading. In reading, people have a much greater access to the world of the imagination than I can imagine they can ever have on either television or on computers. So with that I stop and hope the argument continues.

Professor Willard Jacobson,
Teachers College (Science Education)

Hertzberg quoted John Dewey, which is certainly appropriate in these hallowed halls. What I have to say would perhaps be more fitted to the title "Brave New World", because I think that may be what we are entering.

I shall comment on the three elements of learning style that Gibbon mentioned. Most of the remarks that he made resonated very well with my tympanic membrane. I focus on one of them, for example, by asking you to do something for me. Think what you mean by zero degrees. What is zero degrees? Now when you think through the answer to that question, file it away in your cerebral cortex storage system because we shall come back to it. It is a very simple definition. Zero degrees is the freezing point of pure water, isn't it? So one of the ways to find out what zero is would be to put some distilled water into your refrigerator and watch, and at the moment that that water freezes you have zero degrees. Note that I am using Celsius scale here. But probably a few of you put into your cerebral cortex zero a certain point along side it on an old-fashioned thermometer. That too is an operational definition of zero. But I think a much better definition of zero is that it is a certain spot on a curve that is drawn on a computer screen when you put a sensor into water that eventually will turn to solid.

Here we have three different operational definitions of zero. I would argue that the last one, which may have been in a few cerebral cortexes, is perhaps a more useful operational definition of zero Celsius because you can do more with it. With the technology that we are discussing, I think we are able to do more with it. In many of our high-school laboratories, we are no longer taking zero all the time with a glass thermometer that breaks at least once every laboratory session. In one of the high schools I visited recently there were 128 micro-processors, many of them being used in high-school laboratories, collecting data in different, better ways. It leads me to believe that perhaps we are having a technology that will be with us for a long time. So that's one aspect of learning style. I have three that I comment on.

A second one is that I think we need how to learn to use this technology. The ways we are using it now in most cases is not utilizing all the possibilities that the technology offers us. One thing that Gibbon did not include in his list of characteristics of the curricula was a very, very important one in mathematics and science. How do you make the most out of mathematics and science? I would argue that in part at least you must have many, many experiences in playing with ideas. Now Hawkins once wrote a very famous article in my field called *Messing Around.* His argument was that in the very early elementary-school grades, children should have many experiences, just messing around with materials. I would argue that in early adolescence, in late adolescence, and among adults, all of us should have many opportunities to play around with ideas. The computer makes that more possible, can help us to play around with ideas. If you want to learn mathematics, not arithmetic, you probably have to have experiences in playing around with ideas. If you want to learn science, not just cookbook science, but real science, you also have to have rich experiences in playing around with ideas. You have to take a look at that computer-enriched, computer-shaded picture of the Mojave Desert and be critical, try to understand what it is. You see something. Is it really the Mojave Desert? Well, you say no it is not. Then take a look at the National Geographic. It probably has a beautiful picture of the Mojave Desert too. Is that really the Mojave Desert? Both are very important. Our children need these opportunities to play around with ideas if we aim high.

Just one more point. It seems to me that a lot of our research in science education suggests that if you want children to learn the cognitive dimension of science you should structure the experiences. Apparently, many young people and adults need structure in order to learn the cognitive dimensions of science. I suggest however that if we also want our children to have experiences of playing around with ideas then we should begin to teach them how to use the new technology. I think perhaps the failure of making it possible for our children to utilize the potentialities of the technology is in part because they have never really learned how to use the computer. That it seems to me is one of the kinds of things that we need to teach in the very near future.

Technology and the Curriculum: Promise and Peril

Diane Ravitch
Teachers College,
Columbia University

As an historian discussing the impact of technology on the curriculum, I feel compelled to declare at the outset that I am neither a technophobe nor a technophile. I freely confess that my entire life is bounded by technology, and that I am dependent on its benefits. I cannot imagine life without the automobile, telephone, elevator, flush-toilet, radio, and television. I wrote my presentation on a word processor; I switched from typewriting to word processing 5 years ago. When I travel, I often carry a lap-computer in my briefcase. Much as I love writing on my machines, I must admit that I do not know how to program them or how to use most of their capabilities. I shudder to recall the times that I lost copy, usually because of my own all-too-human errors. I will never forget the night that my teenage son awakened me at 3 a.m. with a haunted look on his face; he did not need to say a word. I knew. He made a mistake; something went wrong; a glitch; he had lost the essay he had been working on all night. As a kind and loving mother, I did not torment him with the inevitable question: "Honey, why didn't you save?" Such are the terrible experiences that presumably build character in the age of the microcomputer.

Most people who have thought much about the impact of technology on modern society feel compelled to choose sides. Any amount of time spent browsing through the very sizable literature on technology reveals the powerful distrust that many intellectuals have for technology. Some writers refuse to use a word processor, for fear that the computer will somehow process not just their language but their very way of thinking. A stalwart few refuse to own a television set, not wanting to become captives of the blue tube. In *The Technological Society,* Ellul (1973) articulated the unease and anxiety felt by so many modern intellectuals when they think about their dependence on machines and standardized processes. More than 20 years ago, he warned that "technique" had become autonomous, that it had penetrated "the deepest recesses of the human being," (p. 325) that it shaped man's environment, and that man in technological society was being reduced to a state of joyous serfdom.

I imagine that those who are working on the frontiers of electronic learning must grow tired of hearing intellectuals complain about the relentless advance of technology. For example, a recent review in *The New York Times Book Review* described E.M. Forster's fear for the future of the human spirit. He wrote:

> The Human Spirit will survive until it becomes non-human: that is to say until the discoveries and inventions we are increasingly making react upon us so strongly that they change our characters. We could no more understand that evolved human race than the monkeys can understand us. (p. 11)

If it is any consolation, writers have been predicting the destruction of the human spirit by the onslaught of the machine ever since the beginning of the Industrial Revolution. One need only recall such films as "The Island of Dr. Moreau," "Frankenstein," or "2001" in order to realize that the theme of technology run amuck has been a persistent theme in fiction and popular culture.

Counterposed to the pessimists who warn about the dangers of technology are the cheerleaders who promise that technology will usher in a revolution of the human condition. In the future, we are led to believe, all of humanity's age-old problems will be vanquished by a combination of human intelligence and technological marvels. Technological progress holds the key, we continue to hope, to banishing war, sickness, poverty, and illiteracy, the age-old scourges of humanity.

If the public seems inclined to believe the prophets of gloom rather than the prophets of unbounded progress, it is because the public understands the fears of the naysayers without trusting the promises of the optimists. Many people are suspicious of the technological revolution; they want the creature comforts that it promises, but they do not understand the new technical jargon, nor do they welcome the idea that some unknown force or elite group is rearranging their society and their future. Even well-educated people discover that they have been turned into techno-peasants, unable to comprehend what the scientists and engineers are doing and powerless to affect the rapid flow of change.

What should the schools do to ease the transition to the age of technology? How will the age of technology affect the curriculum? Will the electronic classroom prove to be a fad like so many other innovations in the past? These are not abstract speculations; they are immediate problems that administrators, curriculum developers, policymakers, and teachers are presently struggling to resolve. At the very least, the rapid changes in the workplace and in the larger society require that we prepare students to understand the complicated and dangerous world that they are about to enter. More than ever, all students need a rich and balanced curriculum that includes a well-developed, sequential program in history, literature, science, mathematics, and the arts. A patchwork curriculum, pieced together from fleeting student interests and curricular fads, will no longer do. Our students need an education for understanding.

What is the place of technology in the schools today? It is clear that the availability of computers for instructional purposes is widespread and growing. As the price of microcomputers has fallen, American schools have been quick to purchase them. By early 1985, 92% of secondary schools had at least one instructional computer, as did 82% of elementary schools; the average secondary school had 13 such machines, and the average elementary school had 5 (Cuban, 1986). In recent years, a number of states have mandated "computer literacy" as a requirement for high-school graduation, which gives the computer a protected status that previous technological innovations never enjoyed.

The history of efforts to introduce new technologies into the schools is not encouraging. In 1913, Thomas Edison predicted, "Books will soon be obsolete in the schools. Scholars will soon be instructed through the eye. It is possible to touch every branch of human knowledge with the motion picture" (Cuban, 1986, p. 11). In his history of machines in the classroom, Cuban says that film never fulfilled its promise, because of the problems of using the equipment, the cost of buying and maintaining it, and the difficulty of finding the right film for the class. Another new frontier for learning was radio; although there were many outstanding examples of educational radio programming in the 1930s and 1940s, the radio never became a regular fixture in the classroom. Instructional television, a much-heralded innovation of the 1950s, also had limited success, in part because of scheduling problems and cost.

Outside the schools, film, radio, and television enjoyed tremendous success, but inside the schools, the textbook continued to be the dominant instructional tool. In every instance, there were reasons, having to do with the cost of the equipment or the training of the teacher or the availability of appropriate programming. Whatever its limitations, the textbook had a certain comforting familiarity; it was always the same, did not require the teacher to have special training, never broke down, never had to be scheduled nor shared with other teachers.

Despite the difficulty of integrating new forms of technology into the classroom, the expectation that schools would finally bow to technological change never ebbed. Gross and Murphy (1964) published a collection of essays called *The Revolution in the Schools,* in which they described the coming "industrialization" of the schools. The editors predicted that the widespread introduction of new technologies—like programmed learning, instructional television, teaching machines, and computers—would bring about "the rationalization and mechanization of the instructional process . . . in American education during the coming decade" (p. 9). With hindsight, it appears thus far that only the computer has found the acceptance and legitimacy that Gross and Murphy anticipated, although it has thus far not challenged the textbook as the dominant instructional tool.

Why did the computer make headway as an instructional tool where film, radio, and television failed? My guess is that the computer has distinctive advantages over the other media as a tool of instruction, because of its possibilities for individualized instruction and interactive learning. Listening to the radio or watching a film or a television program is essentially a passive, group activity; the program will continue even if the members of the audience are asleep or inattentive. The computer, however, does not have an "audience," it has "users," and it demands the user's active participation. Unlike the other media, the user's activity can affect what happens on the screen. At the most superficial level, the computer is an exciting toy on which people can play games of skill and luck; in their most sophisticated applications, computers provide powerful systems for storage and retrieval of information, making them essential in the functioning of the modern mass society.

If the arrival of the electronic classroom is just beyond the horizon—and history should caution us not to be too sure in our assumptions—the schools will enjoy certain benefits, but must also be aware of implicit dangers. My picture of the electronic classroom is possibly inaccurate, but what I have in mind is a classroom utilizing computers, videocassette recorders, videotext, and interactive television. Whether in one classroom or several, I imagine an educational video arcade, where children are learning language, science, or mathematics as they might now play "Space Invaders" or whatever the latest chase-and-destroy game is.

The educational potential of such a classroom is enormous. The most obvious benefit of the electronic classroom is that it achieves what progressive educators could only dream of: a union of work and play. No one continues to believe that learning has to be hard and unpleasant in order to be valuable; if children enjoy learning a foreign language or performing scientific experiments, then they are likelier to be motivated to continue their learning without adult supervision. The prospect of a joyful classroom, where children eagerly seek to learn more, has tantalized and eluded educational reformers for the past century. There is no certainty that the electronic classroom will actually fulfill that promise, but it is this hope that makes its realization so attractive.

Computers have already proven their value even within the context of traditional classroom instruction. The computer is especially useful for drill-and-practice routines, which frees the classroom teacher to assist individuals or small groups. Where appropriate, self-paced instruction allows students to progress at their own rate, using the computer to test their mastery at each step along the way. Also, computers are outstanding in the teaching of writing, whatever the subject area; word-processing programs eliminate drudgery from the laborious task of handwriting, while encouraging students to revise their work without fear of copying the whole thing over. The ability of schools to utilize computers for these purposes entirely depends on their availability; the more computers a school has, the more easily they will fit into classroom life as a supplement to the teacher's tasks.

The new technology has proven its worth in other ways. In Virginia, a demonstration school beams interactive televised classes to far-flung districts. This enables rural districts with few pupils to receive courses like physics; the pupils can participate in the lesson and converse with the teacher. This approach solves two problems simultaneously: It supplies specialized teachers to districts too small to support them as full-time teachers, and it imaginatively overcomes the perennial shortage of teachers in the natural sciences.

The promise of the new technology is dazzling, more dazzling than any of its unsuccessful predecessors. The areas of the curriculum where its promise is brightest are science and mathematics, where problems can be demonstrated visually and where students can employ interactive devices to try out alternative solutions. The new technology fits well with these subject areas because it is not an abstract representation of science and mathematics: It is science and mathematics in action.

Similarly, the curriculum in the arts can be vastly enriched by the new technology, whenever the software catches up with the potential of the hardware. Through videocassettes, which are relatively inexpensive and easy to handle, young people should have ready access to performances of the world's greatest concerts, operas, and dances. Instead of seeing pictures in books of great works of art or architecture, they should be able to take a guided tour of the great museums and historical sites. The schools should remain responsible for active student participation in the arts, providing facilities for painting, dancing, sculpting, film-making, and so on, but the new technologies can bring students to an intimate encounter with the best in each field.

The new technology holds an ambivalent promise for the fields of literature and history, which are the primary humanistic subjects. At present, the software available in these areas is limited. Drill-and-practice is of minimal value to the teacher of literature or history. But there are ways in which these subjects would benefit by the introduction of new technology, particularly if the equipment is technically simple and if the cost of software is low enough so that every school can be well equipped. The teaching of literature would be enriched, for example, if every school had a video library of great plays and films. Students and teachers could select at will from great performances of the works of Shakespeare, Ibsen, Strindberg, Brecht, or from outstanding films, such as those that illustrate the nature of popular culture or the history of film or the work of great directors, writers, and actors.

Teachers of history and social studies also stand to benefit by the introduction of the new technology. The teaching of history would be greatly enriched by the ready availability of relevant visual materials, both to build motivation and to expand learning resources beyond the textbook. Early in 1986, the first video encyclopaedia became available for school use. Imagine the resources available to the teacher who can quickly pull out a videotape on World War II, McCarthyism, the Kennedy years, the civil rights movement, or world leaders like Mao, Churchill, Gandhi, and Stalin.

Similar documentary materials would enhance the teaching of global studies or area studies. Instead of reading a textbook description of a country like India or Brazil, students should be able to observe on a videocassette its people and places, its social and economic problems; they should be able to visit its historic sites, its museums, its cities, its back alleys, its farms, its factories, and its village marketplaces. Many such videotapes already exist, having been shown once or twice on television and then relegated to permanent storage.

But stop. The picture I paint is too bright. Videotape can capture parts of history and literature, but only parts. In history, not everything worth knowing has been filmed. We can give students a dramatic visualization of the war in Vietnam, but not the Civil War. We can show highlights of the administration of Lyndon Johnson, but we cannot portray the trial of Andrew Johnson. Even where there is a wealth of film, the pictures may not capture the most important trends and events, some of which were not known at the time and some of which may not have a visual dimension. As thoughtful news producers know, stories with the best visuals may be without lasting significance, like a three-alarm fire, while the most important developments—major economic news, demographic changes, or basic social change—cannot be filmed, except in a superficial manner. How do you put into pictures the significance of the changing composition of the family or the changing participation of women in the work force? Two or three families may be interviewed, but the presentation is really no better than a textbook discussion, and possibly even less informative.

In the teaching of history, there is a danger that reliance on exciting visuals may distort the curriculum. The plight of the history curriculum in the electronic age may be likened to the dilemma of the drunk who searched for his missing house-keys in the glow of a street light. When asked by a passerby why he kept searching when it was obvious that his keys weren't there, the drunk replied, "I'm looking here because that's where the light is." In an effort to hold their students' attention, teachers of history may find that their decisions about what to teach are shaped by the new media. First, teachers may be tempted to structure the history course to take advantage of the most entertaining electronic materials, instead of focusing on the non-visual causes and effects of the events portrayed. Second, the visuals may influence teachers to place undue emphasis on recent events and to neglect or pass quickly over relatively remote periods, because of the abundance of rich video materials for the past few decades. In either instance, the content of the course would be dictated by the medium, with the ironic effect of limiting the curriculum to those things that were captured on film. One of the purposes of teaching history is to show students the connections between the present and the past, but this would prove impossible if the "past" reaches back only as far as the visual resources permit.

Perhaps the gravest danger of the new electronic media for the teaching of history and literature is that they are implicitly biased against print. Unfortunately, many champions of the electronic classroom like to boast about the superiority of the new technology over the arcane skill of reading. They claim that the electronic media are more democratic than books, because the video screen provides instant access to the viewer, without having to master a special code.

This is a dangerous argument. It is dangerous, first, because our society will become less democratic if print literacy becomes the exclusive possession of elites; our vision of a classless society will be increasingly distant from reality if the schools buy the spurious claim that reading is obsolescent. Secondly, it is wrongheaded to suggest that the electronic media will supplant print technology; they will not. Both must be recognized as vital means of learning, possessing different strengths and performing different functions. Ideally, they should be complementary in the curriculum, not competitive. Just as it would be foolish for booklovers to ignore the value of computers and videocassettes as learning devices, it is equally foolish for advocates of the electronic classroom to scorn the written word.

Perhaps the greatest danger of the new technology is that its very existence tends to devalue printed materials, just as candy and potato chips devalue their more nutritious competitors by surface appeal. If children can choose between playing "Space Invaders" and reading a book, how many will read a book? The answer is already evident in the comparisons of the number of hours that children spend watching television and the amount of time spent reading. Until research answers our questions, we can only wonder whether the new technology develops an insatiable appetite for instant gratification. What happens to people's capacity to analyze materials that do not produce instant gratification? Will we produce a generation imbued with the concept, "If at first you don't succeed, change the channel?"

More perhaps than science and mathematics, the curriculum in history and literature will suffer if print materials are ignored or minimized. In teaching history, visual materials are valuable, but they can never be more than illustrative or suggestive, because they cannot portray causes, trends, or effects. Good history teachers must draw on a variety of sources, such as letters, diaries, newspaper accounts, and autobiographies. Sometimes print materials actually have more drama and immediacy than visual materials. *The Diary of Anne Frank,* for example, is a powerful memoir; no dramatization can be as effective as the diary itself, because Anne wrote the diary in her own words and speaks through it directly to the reader. This is an instance where a visual representation is less immediate and less real than a book.

Whether the topic is recent or remote, students must be able to read in order to understand history as a record and history as a discipline. Pictures can go just so far; the events on the video screen are subject to a variety of interpretations, but students never have available to them the footage that ended up on the cutting room floor or another filmmakers' version of the same events. Film presents only one version of events: what was seen by the camera. The study of history, however, requires that students see events from a variety of angles. When students learn that historians disagree, they also must learn to weigh arguments and evidence, much of which will be drawn from documents, laws, court decisions, and other written materials.

The visual medium and the written language are simply different; they serve different purposes. One cannot take the place of the other. Film offers provocative and illustrative images, but print is necessary for thoughtful analysis. Serious historians require print; their evidence, their argument, their speculation, and their interpretations can be presented fully only in a written language. The use of print gives the historian far more latitude than the use of film; the historian can be imaginative or pedestrian, can draw on examples from across the centuries or appeal to abstract reason, can pick holes in someone else's argument, or can offer alternative explanations. The historian who works with film is limited to what is in the archive. For the historian, the philosopher, the social scientist, the novelist, and the poet, written language is a fuller, richer, and more flexible means of expression than the electronic media.

Prophets of the electronic classroom too often fail to recognize that there are times when visualization is inferior to print. In literature, for example, certain genres were meant to be read, not performed. Novels, short stories, essays, and poems were written to be read. (Some poems, like Vachel Lindsay's, were written to be performed, and others, like *The Illiad,* were originally sung, but they are exceptions.) It will not do to say that students should see dramatizations of novels; the movie of *Great Expectations* is not the same as the novel that Dickens wrote. The novel is a classic, because of its wit and style; the movie is no more than a representation of the real thing. Walt Disney's *Cinderella* is a pallid and saccharine representation of the original folktale.

There are forms that lend themselves to visualization, like plays, dances, songs, and events (when a camera happened to be present). And movies are as much a genre as is the short story or the poem. But there are forms that can only be appreciated when they are read. Any curriculum that did not teach students to appreciate both visual and literary genres, in their original and authentic state, would be deficient.

Will the electronic classroom be an unfriendly environment for the teaching of novels and poems? Will children weaned on "Sesame Street," "Halloween, Part 3," "Dynasty," and "Pac-Man" have the patience to discover the intimate joys of reading great novels, both classic and contemporary? Will their experience of interacting with a blinking, moving screen prevent them from enjoying the very different experience of entering into the imaginative world of an author? Will writers like Coleridge, Millay, Austen, Eliot (George and T.S.), Emerson, Hawthorne, Melville, Dreiser, Whitman, Frost, Auden, and Ellison become as obscure as Tacitus and Plautus? This is the precipice to which the enemies of print literacy seem to be driving us.

One often hears, as an argument for the computer, that the user is empowered because of its interactive capabilities. I argue that the great work of fiction is even more interactive than the computer. The computer, after all, is limited by its program. A far more personal and intense interaction takes place between a reader and a powerful novel, story, or poem. Teachers and literary critics have long recognized that fiction carries different messages to different readers, depending on their life experience. It has often been said that when you read a great book, the book reads you. Depending on their own backgrounds, readers will take different meanings from the novels of Tolstoy, Balzac, or George Eliot. Great poetry has the same power to speak to us in different ways at different points in our lives. No pre-designed program, not even the original intentions of the author, can prescribe limits to the cognitive and affective responses of the reader.

But let us now be candid about the current impact of the new technology on the curriculum. Few schools, if any, have the budget to equip every class-room with computers and video screens. Most schools have a computer room, where students learn simple programming; and most have one or several videocassette recorders. Some districts, fearful that whatever hardware they buy will quickly become obsolescent, have proceeded cautiously in their purchases. Others say they are waiting for the quality of educational software to improve. Houston, Texas, is one of the few school districts to launch a districtwide commitment to educational technology; the district has a department of technology, with its own campus (a former school), its own software developers, a training program for teachers, a library of software, and a staff to evaluate new programs. The district has moved in this direction, not only because its leader-ship believes in the future of the new technology, but as a defense against recurring, possibly permanent, shortages of well-trained teachers.

For the overwhelming majority of schools, the new technology has meant developments far more mundane, far less exciting, far less promising for the curriculum. In reality, the new technology has thus far visited upon the schools a plague of standardized tests. At every level of schooling, from first twelfth grade, students and teachers are being deluged with multiple-choice tests. In the early grades, teachers complain that the curriculum consists of little more than worksheets, and the children spend most of their instructional time filling in blanks and circling words, activities that prepare them for the next round of test-taking. To be sure, it is not the new technology that has led us to embrace standardized tests and busywork, but the romance of the new technology (if I may call it that), the promise that it extends as an answer to the persistent problems of education creates a climate in which it becomes easy to confuse standardization with standards.

With the shape of the new technology already apparent, Hutchins (1969) warned that it might make the inherent problems of mass education even worse. "The means of education," he observed, "do more than affect the ends of education: they become ends" (p. 95). The promise of the new technology, he recognized, was that it would simplify the process of training and the transmission of information; this would leave the cultivation of understanding as the major purpose of educational systems. But, remembering that means become ends, Hutchins asked whether the mass application of technology to education might actually inhibit the development of understanding. His view was that the very nature of technology promotes efficiency and standardization. Machines deal very effectively with questions that have only one right answer, he wrote; when the question has many answers, or "where the aim is to teach something other than the answer, such as appreciation, principles, significance, or understanding, a machine finds itself up against highly recalcitrant material" (p. 99). He recognized that the new devices could "extend training, rote learning, entertainment, and the transmission of information" (p. 105) to vast numbers with increased effectiveness and lessened cost; but he feared that they would "reduce discussion . . . promote centralization . . . [and] drive out the teacher" (p. 105). The danger of the technological devices, he warned, was that "they will dehumanize a process the aim of which is humanization. They will confirm, deepen, and prolong the life and influence of the worst characteristics of mass education" (p. 105).

Mead (1966) took a more hopeful view of the implications of the new technology for the schools and for society as a whole. She contended that technological advances are by themselves neutral, and new technology is "just what the civilization in which it is made can make of it" (p. 67). The elimination of "dull, unrewarding, routine, technical tasks" (p. 69), she believed, would free people for the human tasks that only people can do: "caring for children, caring for plants and trees and animals, caring for the sick and the aged, the traveler and the stranger . . . " (p. 69). She contended that this freedom from routine tasks would cause a multiplication of "tasks for human beings to perform humanly . . . " (p. 69). Rebutting those who feared that automation would promote dehumanization, Mead asked rhetorically

> Is it more or less human for mothers and daughters, separated by hundreds of miles, to be able to dial each other cheaply? Is it more or less human to have a machine to help a child review a rote learning lesson, or calculate the milk money, while a trained teacher is free to teach? . . . Is a child who can rent earphones in a museum and walk about

at his own speed more or less human than one herded in a group of 50? (p. 7)

Regardless of our qualms or hopes, there will be no stopping the forward movement of technology. Each new frontier leads to another; concern about the human cost of progress or the risk to values will not deter the headlong rush to innovate, discover, explore, and improve. I would not argue that it should, because the desire to push knowledge and invention to the horizon is quintessentially human, and it holds the promise of improving the quality of life for more people.

As we plunge forward into an era of scientific marvels and information saturation, educators will be responsible for preparing children to understand the new gadgetry. Students need to learn how to operate the new technological devices and to understand their social implications. But technical skills are not enough. As we all learned when the space shuttle Challenger exploded, all of us need to learn how to cope with tragedy; we need the capacity to reflect on our lives at those times when we discover as limitations as human beings. There will be times when technology fails us, or when we misuse our technological toys, or when we grieve without knowing why.

Technology may improve our standard of living, but it cannot help us understand why we live, what makes our lives worthwhile, or why someone we love should die. We need ways to find meaning in a universe that often defies logic and human purpose; we need ways of thinking that will help us interpret the barrage of information that daily overwhelms us. We need to establish our individuality, our *raison d'etre,* in a society that technology makes ever more organized, ever more bureaucratized, and ever more indifferent to simple human courtesies.

The glamour and gimmickry of educational technology must not be permitted to erode the humanistic side of the curriculum, especially the study of history and literature. The study of these disciplines is important, indeed vital, for all of us, because they are records—in most instances, *written* records—of the ways in which other men and women have found meaning in the world. History provides us with a context in which to make sense of the flow of events. Literature provides us with the efforts of other people to find meaning in their lives. If the schools condition children to learn only those things that can be absorbed in the format of a video arcade, with lights flashing and bells ringing, then the teaching of history and literature will suffer.

Doubts will continue to plague us as we embrace the new technology and it embraces us. What are the tradeoffs? Will the teacher have more time to teach or will the teacher play second fiddle to the gadgets? In the summer of 1984, *Forbes* magazine published an extraordinary debate on the significance of the microcomputer in education. When a senior editor wrote an article about the enormous educational potential of computers, the editor of the technology section wrote an internal memo in which he challenged the claim that the computer would transform the way people learn. Wrote the technology editor:

What kind of transformation will computers generate in kids? It could well be a lot less than all the hype would indicate. Just as likely as producing far more intelligent kids is the possibility that you will create a group of kids fixated on screens—television, videogame, or computer. The notion of learning at your own speed is a hoary educational cliche beloved by computer ed folks. In theory it sounds wonderful. In fact, it eliminates the community of the classroom, turns the student into a lone figure engaged in a yearlong dialog with a disembodied voice. What would happen to class discussion—and, more important, the sense of rubbing against other minds?

I think that the best schools will eventually recognize a fact that's been apparent since Plato sat on Socrates' knee: Education depends on the intimate contact between a good teacher—part performer, part dictator, part cajoler—and an inquiring student. The importance of the teacher is not necessarily as a conveyor of information but as a catalyst to interest students in learning for themselves. In the end it is the poor who will be chained to the computer; the rich will get teachers. (pp. 35-40; 4,156)

More likely, the rich will have both teachers and the latest technology.

As we look ahead, we can be sure that technology will solve some of our educational problems and will create others. No one can doubt that it has become a permanent part of American education and that it offers exciting prospects for the classroom. But it is my conviction that technology—no matter how wonderful the machinery—will prove irrelevant in our quest for answers to our greatest need, and that is, to educate the heart, the spirit, and the understanding.

DISCUSSION

Professor Hazel Hertzberg
Teachers College (Social Studies)

I found Professor Ravitch's chapter one with which I am in deep and general sympathy, although not in every detail. I think this has to do with the fact that we are both historians.

As I have tried to think of the major impact so far on the school of the computer (others who have more experience with this may correct me) I think the major impact has been in terms of scheduling. Until we had a computer we could not have mini courses. We could not have modular scheduling, we could not have the kind of curricular fragmentation that developed at the time in which computers entered the school management. That does not mean that you have to blame the fragmentation of knowledge, which was a result of that, on the computer. It would not have happened had there not been other reasons for doing so, although in some schools they tell me that just because the computer is there they want to do something with it. This is an unfortunate use of computers, although I know if I had to do the scheduling, I would certainly welcome one.

In my own field, the materials that I have seen are essentially the junk food of instruction. I have not seen one social studies piece of equipment, on a disk or anything, that does anything but muck up people's minds. For example, one of the early ones I saw is very amusing and it was developed by a teacher. This was a way of teaching geography: a certain ship set out under sail from southern Europe at the behest of a certain queen. The captain was an Italian (there wasn't any name given to this ship), and all along the crew decided (naming the children in the class) what would be the latitude and longitude of the ship in order get themselves to some place called the New World. I am sure that was a good way to learn latitude and longitude. But it is not a good way to learn the conditions on a sailing ship in the 1500s, or indeed today. Crews do not vote on latitude and longitude. An important social structure in our society is thereby distorted and it is ridiculous for children to be taught that way. I think many of the simulations are of this nature.

Secondly, I want to reiterate a point that Professor Ravitch made and that is that all sources, including the computer, have to be looked at critically. We don't do nearly enough of this in schools. We don't subject any of the news reports, textbooks, all the kinds of sources that people use, to enough critical review by students. I think we have to develop particular ways that are appropriate to analyse the material that comes over the computer. But we have to do it. The computer has a kind of cachet that may put it beyond criticism and that would be wrong.

I want to repeat that the history of technology should be a very critical part of instruction in history and that only by seeing this particular blip on the historical process will we understand its place: where it came from, its roots, the intellectual roots, the social roots, its possible impact on society. If we don't have that kind of historical perspective, I see no possibility of us understanding it very well or managing it. We have to understand that the computer also has a viewpoint. It is not a neutral agency. The computer is a selector, the computer is a purveyor, the computer is no more a neutral agency than is a book. We have had many calls for the history of technology in the social studies and not enough attention to them. John Dewey favored this because he felt that if people were going to manage machines, instead of visa versa, that they had to know the history of the impact of technology on society, and also the impact of science, because Dewey regarded science, perhaps much more optimistically than we would today, as a liberator of the human mind. The great historian, James Harvey Robinson advocated the same thing. Now this was early in this century and we haven't gotten very far in integrating that into our curriculum.

I also want to urge that much more attention be paid to research on learning. What is the impact on learning complex subjects like history and literature? What is the effect of the computers on that? That is very difficult to assess. It seems obvious to me, that the perceptions of time and space that our students have, have been fundamentally altered by television. Their links with the past have been broken, much more than before television. They are focussed on processes and they have little real genuine conception of how processes actually work. For example, they don't know how a news program on television is put together. It simply appears magically, and nobody discusses it with them. They have no opportunity to find out how that works. Similarly I fear that certain kinds of learning will take place at the computer without it being subjected to the kind of critical scrutiny that it should. So those agencies that are concerned with the spread of computers should also be very much concerned about the impact on children of computer instruction.

Professor Willard Jacobson, Teachers College (Science Education)

I continue to use as my text, the "Brave New World." A central idea I discuss is that, we should, we must, we will continue to try out, experiment with, fail, succeed, in the use of technology in our schools. We should do it, we must do it, we are going to do it, and we need to study it as we go along. I am not an historian, so I tread into history with some trepidation, although I have never hesitated. I suggest that the experiences that we have had with television, educational television, support the central idea I develop. Then I also mention some of the Japanese experience that seems to me to be pertinent.

A number of years ago I went down to, I think it was Maryland, and saw the schools all wired up for television. Also I went to the mid-West and I saw television programs that came down from an airplane that circled over Ohio everyday to generate signals that could be picked up throughout the mid-West. I think it is fair to say that these experiments were not successful. You no longer see an airplane flying over the middle West, although satellites do and we get many of our television programs that way. Now we have learned that there are better ways to use television. The videotape recorder, the videotape player, gives us much more flexibility, makes available for one child or a hundred children, experiences that they would not have any other way. The point is that we learned, we learned from those abyssmal failures in the middle West and in Maryland how better to use educational television. We need to experiment with technology. We need to continue.

We have just finished a monograph of analysis and comparison of science education in Japan and the United States. I will only refer to their experiences with the computer. They are not going about it the way we are. They are not going to put computers into schools, according to their writings. They are not going to put computers into schools until they have the kind of hardware that they are sure will persist and even more important, until they have the software that they want for their children to use. That is all very fine. But it seems to me that a pertinent question is, where are they going to learn about what works and what doesn't work? Where are they going to learn and obtain the software that works? They'll probably get it in the United States. My co-author, Professor Takamura from Hiroshima University, says the genius of Japan is to be able to locate good ideas, bring good ideas back to Japan, adapt them to their society and then use them in their society. This is the Japanese way of doing things. I suggest the American way is quite different. Our way, at least in part, involves experimentation, research, development, study, historiography. We try things, we do things. Some of them fail. But I hope that with each of the failures, we move a little bit forward. I really am all for the printed word. I have written a number of books, and I hope people keep buying them.

Much of what Ellul says is sheer, pure unadulterated nonsense. But, nobody is better than Ellul at evoking ideas. He is well worth reading because of that. Don't read him to believe him. Read him to improve the ideas that you have. It seems to me that is one of the major functions of writing. Many of us like to communicate. There's another function of that, that is to write, to stimulate, to evoke, to help the reader to reach ideas he or she would not reach unless somebody like Ellul put it down, in this case, on paper. The central idea again is, it seems to me, we need to, we must, we are going to experiment with the computer, experiment with technology, some of it will fail, some of it will succeed. Probably most of it will be very drastically changed. That, it seems to me, is part of the great educational adventure in which all of us are a part.

REFERENCES

Ellul, J. (1973). *The technological society.* New York: Knopf.

The *New York Times Book Review,* February 23, 1986, p. 11.

Cuban, L. (1986). *Teachers and machines: The classroom use of technology since 1920.* New York: Teachers College Press.

Gross, R., & Murphy, J. (Eds.). (1964). *The revolution in the schools.* New York: Harcourt, Brace & World.

Hutchins, R. M. (1969). *The learning society.* New York: Mentor Books. p. 95, 99, 105.

Margaret Mead, M. (1966). The challenge of automation to education for human values In W.W. Brickman & S. Lehrer (Eds.), *Automation, education, and human values* (pp. 67-70). New York: School and Society Press. p. 67, 69.

Forbes, August 13, 1984, pp. 35-40; August 27, 1984, pp. 4, 156.

3

Information and Imagery Education

Mary Alice White
Teachers College,
Columbia University

In this chapter I make six statements about what I see as the fast-changing world of information, as opposed to an unchanging world of education, and the problems coming from that lack of fit.

My views are simply put:

1. The world of information is changing quickly, deeply, and widely, presenting us with the need to redefine and to rethink the nature of information itself.

2. Part of that change in information is a shift from print to imagery as the medium for information delivery, transformation, and exchange.

3. The change in information itself, and the shift to imagery, is affecting deeply how we see our world, how we think about it, and therefore how we behave toward it.

4. The technologies should be viewed as the instruments for change that they are, but we as educators should be thinking more about their impact on learning and on society.

5. Education, by which I mean particularly public education, K–12, does not recognize the seriousness of these changes in information and in imagery. If these changes were taken as seriously as they should be, they would require us to rethink the heart of education itself. Instead, education is treating the technologies as just another adjunct to the traditional triad of textbook, teacher, and test.

6. In my view, the changes we are undergoing are so significant for how we learn, how we remember, and how we form judgments that I believe education needs to develop a curriculum designed to educate for these changes.

Let me try to explain my reasons for these six statements. My first statement was that the world of information is changing quickly and deeply and widely, presenting us with the need to redefine and to rethink the nature of information itself.

We live in a world where 50% of those who work in offices are using computers in their work. Robots are helping to make many of our industrial products. Satellite receivers dot the landscape; compact disks are here for music and word storage; and optical fiber delivery systems, we are told, are just around the corner when it will be possible to receive and send voice, data and text, moving and still pictures, and graphics on the screen or downloaded to hard copy. New York's Governor Mario Cuomo has proposed laying such an optical fiber network along that state's highway system, and recommended to the New England governors recently that an optical fiber network should be the priority for the New England states. Around the corner may be here this year. I think everyone familiar with the technologies agrees that we will soon pass through the chaos we are now experiencing into a melding of all the components into one integrated system of video—phone—computer-

If we look at the changes in the home and the school, the home is far ahead of the school. There is a computer in one out of seven households, some of which are in use. Videocassette recorders (VCRs) will be in one out of every three homes this year. The entertainment industry has changed drastically. This year, Hollywood will have earned more from cassettes than from movie theaters. Television, that ubiquitous technology, now reaches 2.5 billion people in 162 countries, which makes it the largest educational system in the world. *Live Aid,* the TV music benefit for starving African families was seen by one-quarter of the world's population—surely the most watched event in human history!

And what is happening to school age children in all this? They certainly watch MTV; they listen to taped music; they watch television 4-5 hours a day; they listen to the radio almost everywhere; they love the VCR and its movies; and any time that is left over during the day, they spend in talking to their friends in person or on the telephone—and maybe listening to their teachers, and maybe reading from a textbook. We would be very foolish not to recognize that young people today are familiar with ways of communicating that were not even invented when we were in school. Students, for example, get 75% of all their news from a television screen, not from print.

I argue strongly that the significant political information—what decides elections—comes from electronic imagery. It does not come from print. It is the campaign video clips on the nightly news, and the paid political videos, that require a new kind of literacy, what I call "imagery comprehension." I return to this point shortly.

My second and third statements were that part of this change in information is a shift from print to imagery as the medium for information delivery, transformation, and exchange, and that the change in information itself, and the shoft to imagery, is affecting deeply how we see our world, how we think about it, and therefore how we behave toward it. Let me explain these two points together.

For 10,000 years, humans learned from images and from speech. For the last 500 years, humans have learned primarily from print. In the future, humans may learn primarily from electronic imagery. Is this electronic imagery a new way of learning and communicating? Or are we going back to old ways of learning? I argue that electronic imagery is not only a new way of learning, but that it may develop into a new way of thinking about our world.

Humans have used a variety of images to record events, to celebrate heroes and gods, to memorialize a society's history and culture. We have created images through statues, paintings, mosaics, architecture, pottery, carvings, stained glass, and coins. These images have served as a language of learning for a non-literate people by communicating images they could hold in their heads. They created a memory bank of implicit values, ideals, and religious rules that would guide behavior and thinking. "Reading" the stone carvings on a medieval church provided memorable lessons from the Bible. Statues on the Acropolis acted as an image memory bank to remind the viewer of the power and glory of the gods. In public places, statues to victorious leaders reminded the viewer of an illustrious defeat of the enemy, or of sacrifices made against impossible odds as at Thermopylae. We humans have created rock paintings of a deer hunt from the prehistoric period; numerous paintings of scenes during the Trojan War: statues of Alexander; mosaics of Empress Theodora; hundreds of images of the crucifixion in every possible medium; parables from the Bible in stone, in wood, in wool, in glass, in paint; and coins showing the heads of state, warriors, and martyrs.

Our history, as a species, overflows with images we have created to tell a story to be remembered.

REMEMBERING IMAGES

Remembering electronic images is a psychological process we know little about. Psychologists disagree about how we store images, largely because there is no direct way to find out. We cannot open up the top of someone's head to peer into their memory storage to see if it contains one chamber, as it were, for words, another for images, another for music, and another for speech. Psychologists have had to study memory by inference. One theory by Paivio (1971) holds that there are two memory storage processes, one for words and one for images, and that when the brain receives an item to remember, it will store its word version (e.g., "red barn") in the word storage area, and the image (of a "red barn") in the image area, so that there is "dual processing" of those items that contain both words and images. Some psychologists argue that our memory is organized in a computer-like storage area, reduced to some sort of binary system that can be instructed to recall both words and images on demand. Other psychologists feel that all of our information, including images, is stored in word form. Still other psychologists contend that there are several systems of memory, including one system that stores images received through our vision and senses (external images) and another system for storing images generated internally (Bower, 1983). Experiments have demonstrated by inference that humans can manipulate images in their head in making comparisons of size, reducing the image, and enlarging the image (Kosslyn, 1980). Humans appear to be able to hold an image in their head and move it around in fairly complex ways, something artists, architects, and engineers probably do quite often without questioning how it is done.

Our notion of how human memory works is being greatly influenced by advances in computer technology. Some cognitive psychologists keep trying to make their models of the human brain operate like a computer, whereas some artificial intelligence researchers keep trying to make their computer operate like the human brain. As the technology develops, so do the theories. Computers are moving from *serial processing*, (which means that the computer handles information only in one step after the other, "serially" or seriatim) to *parallel processing* (which means that computers will be able to handle information along different routes simultaneously, along "parallel" roads). Psychologists like Pribram (1985) argue that our nervous system works much more in parallel than serially, and that, in fact, the human brain can call up information from memory by its content (parallel processing) rather than by where it is located (serial processing).

As information technology becomes even more complex, we may discover how images are stored in memory and how they influence our thinking and behavior. Our theories of human memory, some would say, are much too imitative of how computer technology works; while the opposing argument is that computer technology will make possible experiments that will reveal how the human brain processes information. If it is true that our theories of human memory are deeply influenced by advances in computer technology, it it possible that as the technology moves from being print oriented to being image oriented, that our theories of human memory will also become much more image oriented.

LEARNING FROM IMAGES

But it is clear that humans are able—somehow—to store images in their memory, as well as words, and to recall them as images and as words.

But is the process of learning from images different from learning from print? Does it make any difference whether a student remembers Franklin Roosevelt from seeing an electronic image of him or from reading his name in a book? There lies a coming debate in psychology and education.

When we learn from print, we learn in a structure formed by the technology of the printing press, although we may not be aware of it. We read print from left to right, from the top to the bottom, and turn a page. Not only is the layout of the information structured by the medium of print, but more importantly, the organization of that information. When we instruct students to "take notes," what we really mean is "organize your information according to print." That means we have headings, starting with an overall heading, then in finer detail with sub-headings as we go down, ending with a summary paragraph. What god ever ordered information to be organized in a vertical linear fashion? It has become such an accepted custom so that we assume information is inherently vertical, left, right, and linear. This is a dangerous assumption.

Compare for a moment, how that same news story is structured on the nightly television news program. Do we see a vertical linear structure? No, we do not. We see an opening image, usually a videotape clip from that day's filming; hear the voice of the newsperson; and see the image of that anchorperson seated at a desk reading (note, "reading") the news from an unseen prompter. We see all these images on a flat rectangular plane, called a *screen.* In print, we have a linear sequence that moves, at least theoretically, from an overview, through detail, to a summary. On television news, we have a sequence that is dictated by the availability of appropriate videotape, and a story written to be heard. There is no obvious order except for the order of the news stories, which take their lead from the headlines of leading daily newspapers.

In print, the lines are static. In electronic imagery (on television, on videotape, on computer, on videodisc)—the images are moving.

In print, the sequence of information is dictated by the technology of the press, which has led to an accepted structure that is vertical linearity. In electronic imagery, the sequence may be dictated by the narrative, by the sound or music if it is carrying the story at that moment, or by the images themselves.

Does it make any difference in the way we handle information if the information comes in linear form, or whether it comes in image form? I argue that it could make a critical difference. In linear form, we learn that B follows A, which is essential to grasping logical meaning, so that sequencing is an essential skill for print comprehension. In imagery, the only sequence is the order of cuts on the film, tape, or disc; and that sequence may or may not be essential to comprehension. Imagery comprehension depends on the ability to process images, many of them occurring simultaneously within one frame, which requires an ability to merge (select? organize?) several images together in order to comprehend the total imagery message.

These different ways of learning may have impact on how we think. If we think in terms of linear solutions, we tend to think of A, then B, then C, then D, and so on. If we think in terms of imagery solutions, we may be more inclined to think of relational solutions, in which "A" will set off a ripple effect through an interdependent and interactive system, represented as a system of images.

Think for a moment of a series of filmed images of a countryside, as the camera pans around hills and valleys. That sequence may be dictated by topography and the eye of the cameraperson, not by sequential logic. Think of a very different sequence that can be seen on MTV in which the images jump— literally jump—from a singer's face, to the singer in costume for a fantasy related to the lyrics of the song, jump to a part of the body of the singer, jump to fantasy, jump to dancers, jump to fantasy, and so on. What is that sequence? Some contend it is the most sophisticated use of imagery on any medium today. The imagery itself acts as the stimulus. Your eyes are assaulted by rapid changes of images that hold your attention, that shock, that assault your reason because the images appear to follow no rational sequence. The temporal sequence is reversed or chaotic. You cannot tell what happened in what order, fantasy or song. You are receiving a visual barrage. That visual barrage apparently helps us to remember a series of sounds (remember the opera example) so that we will then be likely to go out and buy those sounds as a record. So here is an example of images being used very purposefully to sell a memory of sound.

LOCUS OF MEMORY SYSTEM

And what principles do those MTV images follow? They follow those ancient principles of remembering images that were laid down in 6th Century B.C. in Greece, revived by the Romans, and employed fairly extensively in the Middle Ages. As the story goes, Simonides, a famous Greek poet and orator, was speaking at a banquet. While he was called outside, the banquet roof fell in, killing all those at the table, so badly that they could not be identified. Simonides was asked if he remembered where each sat, whereupon he recalled accurately the exact order in which each guest had been seated. Simonides was using a well-known memory technique of orators in those days who had no written notes. The orator would imagine a familiar location ("locus") such as a temple, a large building with chambers, or an extensive courtyard. As he imagined this familiar locus the orator would place, in his imagery, the points he wished to make in his speech, starting with the first room, for example, as he walked through this familiar setting, and then to the second, and so on. When the orator rose to speak, he would imagine himself walking through these same spaces and would recall each point in turn. In order to help him remember certain points, he would follow the advice of those who handed down this "locus of memory system," which was to image a scene that was in vivid colors (preferably red), that was in active motion, and which was in someway exaggerated or distorted from its normal appearance. This combination of vivid color, motion, and distortion were thought to be of help in remembering images—as indeed, 20th century psychology has rediscovered, as has MTV.

MTV has gone beyond what Simonides could teach us about the locus of memory system. It has taken the precepts of vividness, movement, and exaggeration, and heightened these with what electronic technology can deliver. We have movement of the performers, movement of the camera, and movement through graphics. We have vividness of colors (and certainly of sound) but also vividness of images that are out of context in space and time, juxtaposed in rapid fire sequence so that the eye and the brain must operate rapidly to make sense out of these fleeting vivid images. Is this a new Simonides, telling us how to make viewers remember images? Do the new rules of Simonides for electronic imagery storage imply that images (a) must be rapid; (b) distort normality, even to the level of the grotesque; (c) contain movement, perhaps including violence; (d) maximize sensual and sexual imagery; (e) utilize vivid colors; and (f) hold the eye with sequences that are perceptually illogical? If so, this is a long way from the printed book, a very long way.

SHAPING OF INFORMATION BY PRINT AND BY IMAGES

Does this suggest that imagery and text shape information in different ways? The electronic image has its rectangular flat plane also but there is no rule, as there is in print, that an image should be read from top to bottom, or from left to right. Images are read in the sequence that is derived from the image's inherent composition that is designed to attract the eye. In moving images, the eye may be attracted by the motion itself from frame to frame. Our view of the world through these images is of a rectangular world, an upright, flat-planed rectangular world, whether we see the image in a photograph, on a TV screen, on a videotape screen, on a computer terminal, or on a videodisc display. The world is upright and rectangular. A book page, we must add, is also usually rectangular, so humans have a very rectangular view of the world from these two major information sources, very different from the circular in-depth view of the human eye.

Sequence

If our view of the world is a flat-planed rectangular one, how does sequence shape information? With text, the reader usually knows where he or she is located in terms of the unfolding of meaning. The opening sentence or paragraph should orient the reader to the substance of the text to follow; each subsequent paragraph deals with a related point or elaboration; the final paragraph sums up the substance. This sequence is typically found in nonfiction writing, which includes most of the reading done by students as part of their schooling. An experienced student can locate the appropriate paragraph for answering those questions posed at the end of the chapter by following this sequence.

Fiction is sequenced in a number of ways, from a straightforward narrative, sequenced by chronology; to the other extreme, organized through the internal mind's eye of the hero or heroine, using as its sequential tie a series of associations that were stored in the subject's memory (speech, sound, music, odor, taste, an incident, a scene, an impression), all of which were employed by writers like Virginia Woolf and Proust and those who followed.

Whichever organizational sequence is chosen, words must follow each other in a prescribed order of left to right, and down a line, and over to the next page.

Images, too, must follow each other, as do words, if they are seen in motion in a series of frames. But they can be superimposed on each other, and dissolved from one to another. Still photos can be exhibited in any sequence, including the shooting sequence, but are usually exhibited with an eye to the content and its visual impact on a walking adult viewer. The narrative may impose sequence on both moving and still images, if the narrative is carried by the images themselves. For example, an adventure narrative on TV must show the action in its appropriate chronology in the images, accompanied of course by appropriate sound and speech. Here the sequence is dictated by which event followed which other event, as shown in the images themselves of the players fighting, chasing, running, and finally catching.

But a visual sequence can be free of narrative demands. A videotape of the changing seasons must follow the order of the seasons, but the narrative may be solely the mood evoked by the imagery. Images then are chosen for their mood-evoking power, more than for their ability to convey seasonal chronology. A visual sequence can also be subservient to the music, or to speech, serving as an amplifier of the information and content suggested by sound. Think for a moment of the national anthem being played over your radio. The image that may leap into your mind is of the American flag, waving in the wind. Here the visual image symbolizes the patriotic mood evoked by the music.

Movement

In text, there is no movement supplied by print, only the movement supplied by the reader's rate of reading. In contemporary imagery, there is a wide exposure to movement created by the camera, from stills to moving pictures, to slowed down speed, to fast forward, to freeze frame, to reverse motion.

Within the images, not only is there the movement supplied by the technology of the camera but movement is also created by the players within the images. That movement can be frenetic, as in MTV; it can be slow; it can appear from right to left, left to right, top to bottom, or bottom to top, or cut diagonally across the screen. Movement in fact can appear anywhere within the image, and go in any direction, even if it defies gravity; and even if it defies the laws of perceptual logic that represent how we have experienced reality in time and space. We do not expect to see a waiter appear at the right of our screen in the first scene, approaching the players' table, and then see him approach from the left, without some visual explanation that the observer (the camera) has changed position. If the camera does change position, it must maintain perceptual logic, so that the second view of the waiter from left must appear to be consistent with what an observer would see had the camera only moved its location. If the scene showed the kitchen's location completely shifted, we, as observers, would feel disoriented and played upon unfairly. But if the subject were clearly a fantasy, then the laws of perceptual logic would be suspended and anything would be permissible.

Color

Color is lacking in most texts, although colored illustrations often accompany text. There is conflicting evidence whether illustrations help readers, especially young readers, to comprehend the text. One interpretation is that illustrations help if they do, in fact, illustrate the text (i.e., clarify its meaning through images). Some illustrations confuse young readers because they suggest a different meaning than the one suggested by the text so that two channels of information compete with each other, one in text, the other in images.

Color is an essential part of most electronic images, on the television screen and on the monitor. When the Macintosh computer was introduced, the cry was "It's not in color!" One cannot imagine that cry being heard about a new book in print. Color is so much part of the new imagery that it is hard to think of those images without thinking of them in color. Graphics are essentially color graphics, whether they display an analysis of a business situation, a fantasy adventure, enhance a tv commercial, or a singer's performance on MTV.

This ubiquitous use of color images raises one of the unanswered but interesting questions about human memory: Is print stored in black and white, but electronic imagery stored in color? If so, what effect does this have on remembering? If Simonides' original idea about the importance of vividness still holds, we would have to deduce that what is stored in color is more likely to be remembered than black and white. When we add the presence of movement to color, which Simonides also stressed, we are making a strong hypothetical case for the superior strength of remembering electronic imagery over static black and white text. (It may be that the advertising industry discovered this long ago.)

USING INFORMATION FROM TEXT AND IMAGERY

If it is true that print and electronic imagery differ considerably in their use of sequence, color, and movement, does this difference shape the information they carry? We have very little evidence to go on, but a reasonable hypothesis is that these differences do matter, that information can be, and is, transformed by color and movement, and that sequence can change the essential nature of information content.

And if we ask whether these differences matter to human learning, we raise of the interesting questions for psychology to answer: Are electronic images, with their color and movement, not better and longer remembered than print? There is reason to think so.

Let us take the example of a student learning a passage from a history text. The student is required to remember a particular historical incident. The incident itself is far from the student's own experience—a battle, a passage of a bill, a change in political power, a revolt. In order to remember it, the student needs to attach the new information to old information, to use some sort of "hook." Information stored in isolation, unconnected to anything previously stored, is extremely hard to recall. The student in this example, has no personal experience he or she can "hook" this passage to, so the student gropes for a hook which is meaningful, such as a similar incident from previous historical reading on which to build a semantic hook; or, lacking a semantic similarity, he or she may try a word association, such as a (hypothetical) "Spanish steps rebellion." He or she makes the association of the word "Spanish" to "Juan" who was king at the time, and "step" he or she makes into an acronym, "s" for slaves; "t" for "tyranny"; "e" for "escape"; "p" for "put down," which helps the student to remember the sequence of events in which certain slaves revolted against tyranny, tried to escape, but the rebellion was put down under the reign of "Juan."

Now let us compare a similar example from imagery. The scene is the steps during the sailors' rebellion from Eisenstein's film, "The Battleship Potemkin." If you have seen this film even once, you are quite likely to recall the scene of the steps as you read these words. It is an unusually vivid scene, beautifully constructed to make its point. But you will notice that you were able to bring up this image by reading words that identified it, so you were moving from words to a stored image.

Now what happens when we go from image to stored image? This is what advertising is all about. The TV commercial tries to put an image into your head of a brand product, and surrounds it with everything enjoyable, tantalizing, and appealing—in spoken words, music, sound, graphics, in the players, in the sequence of events that end up with something positive happening, like a miniature Horatio Alger story—so that the image will be stored with positive feelings. The next time you enter the supermarket or drugstore, the advertiser hopes very much that you will recognize the image of that product, recalling it with positive feelings, and will therefore purchase it. Advertising is aimed at memory for images, skillfully done electronically. A jingle will stay in the viewer's auditory memory, reminding them of the name of a product, and its image. Apparently we can move from words we have stored in our memory, to images, to music, and back and forth—or else advertising efforts have been futile.

But how do we use one image to recall another image? We can use words to recall other words, such as the title of a book that will, for some fortunate souls, bring up the author's name. The title of a legislative act will recall the names of the senators who introduced it. Recalling one impressionist painter's name is likely to bring up another's; and so on. Much of what we learn in school is based on our ability to store words that are meaningful, and then to recall them when we are given one or two key words—on a test, for example, or when a teacher asks a short question. That is how we use our memory in school to learn and to perform.

But what about images, which are almost never used in school as a carrier of learning? If we flash one image on the screen, will the viewer recall another? If so, how are they linked? Are those images linked semantically i.e., one image recalled from "Potemkin" will bring up another? Are they recalled by the setting in which the images were experienced such as recalling seeing "Potemkin" with a friend on a hot July afternoon"? Are they recalled by some kind of "image association," perhaps like word association, in which images that are alike in their appearance can be recalled together? Perhaps this is the kind of image association that some visual artists may have that enables them to recall images of similar appearances? If we can recall "castle; sand; beach" as a word association, what images are associated if we see a photograph of Omaha beach?

IMPLICATIONS FOR INFORMATION

What are the implications of sequence, movement, and color of electronic imagery for the transmission of information? Will we be receiving and utilizing a different type of information? And if so, what are the implications if we have a different information base upon which to operate?

There are five potentially significant changes in information if it is transmitted in image form.

Images are More Transitory than Print.   In the present state of technology, most viewers are not going to keep a record of the images they see on their monitors, such as the evening TV news. If a record if not easily available, then information is less subject to scrutiny and analysis. Misleading images are harder to define, record, and analyze than the printed story. So image information may be more ephemeral than print.

Images Have No Commonly Accepted Standards.   Viewers may be more subjective in their perception of images than they are of print, a point that needs investigation. There are rules for print, partly because we have been formally taught to read; there are words and what they commonly mean, which has been standardized by a dictionary; and there is the English common law, which has interpreted the meaning of English words and phrases for human behavior over the centuries.

There is no dictionary of images that defines what an image means. We have not been taught—unfortunately—how to read images. There is no law based on the meaning of images except a minute beginning in libel TV cases. We have no standard, in short, against which we can compare images for their "true" meaning. An image means what you perceive it to mean, and "you" is the creator as well as the viewer.

The Time Frame of Images is Usually More Immediate than Print.   This is so partially because of the costs involved. Images on television, in particular, are limited in time to 2–3 minutes or less per news story and now 10 and 15 second commercials are appearing. News stories are compressed into what is of immediate news value. There is no time for background, no time for historical perspective.

Images on television entertainment programs compete for the viewers' eyes. They must attract and hold the eye with compelling images. Compelling images tend to be immediate, telling the viewer that this is the latest, the most up-to-date. Compelling images do not include images from the relevant historical background. The tempo is now, this moment. This passion for the latest even extends to print information available on computer data bases. The stock market is affected within seconds by a statement of a Federal Reserve Board chairman, testifying in Washington miles away. Students using a database for writing a story in school communicate with databases that may go back to the 1960s, but this is a very limited historical perspective. So the rage for being current gives us images of information that are very up-to-date, but without perspective.

Visual Images Tend to be Fragmented.   The pressure of limited time also leads to fragmented information—a clip of an image of a face here, an image of a scene there, but none more than a few seconds. Continuity and perspective take time, which costs money. Fragmentation is also a visual technique for holding attention, as on MTV. The same snappy tempo and fragmented images appear in *USA TODAY,* which prints capsule articles, many colored photos, and is dispensed from a television-like box.

Entertaining Images are Blended with Information.   Images on television have to compete for the immediate attention of the viewer in a way that is quite different from print. A book title must compete with other book titles for a purchase, but once purchased, its ability to compete with other concurrent interests of the purchaser goes unrecorded. (Videotapes compete more like books).

Because of the need to compete for attention, images are used as an entertainment device in the delivery of information. Watching an announcer read the news is not very attention-holding, not even on the BBC, although it worked well on a different medium called radio. But now the news information is made as entertaining as possible in order to hold as wide a viewer audience as possible.

At the same time, we are seeing entertainment become one part of the two-part recipe for educational computer software: entertainment and learning. There is nothing inherently wrong with making learning entertaining. In fact, there is everything inherently right about it. Should learning not be fun? Isn't it sensible to make that learning, which is repetitive yet which must be mastered, as much fun as possible so as to motivate the youngster to do it over and over? Of course, but the problem is how to mix the entertainment with the learning so as not to distort the information to be learned. When the quality of the information is sacrificed to entertaining images, then we have information that is entertaining but not educational.

A similar trend is occurring on the tv news programs, fighting to hold their audiences with entertaining news in the face of cable and VCR competition. We have even seen the emergence of a new form, called the *docudrama,* which is neither entertainment nor facts, but an amalgam of both, and the viewer must navigate between them without a chart.

What happens to the notions of accuracy, truth, and objectivity in information when information is processed into entertaining images? The answer is obvious—those notions lose out, at least for a time.

Partly because imagery itself is less standardized than print at this stage of its development; partly because it is often ephemeral at this level of technology; and largely because imagery is a tool being used in visual competition as a fragmentary, immediate, entertaining, eye-holding tool; for these reasons, imagery may transform information, shaped by a print-based carrier with a history of rules for accuracy and objectivity, into information molded by an image-based carrier as an entertainment package with less regard for accuracy and objectivity. (If this happens, we can expect a reaction which eventually will drive imagery into a set of standards for reporting news events, similar to that which has developed for print.)

If the nature of the information we receive is changed, will this affect our view of the world and how we behave in response to it?

WHAT ARE THE IMPLICATIONS FOR HUMAN BEHAVIOR?

It seems reasonable to assume that people operate differently, if given different information. If one believes the world is flat, one is unlikely to sail too far out for fear of falling off the earth.

Will our behavior be affected if we receive visual information that is more ephemeral, immediate, fragmented, more personalized in meaning, and more entertaining in nature than has been true of print over the last 400 years?

Perhaps the most noticeable change will be in *tempo.* If information arrives in short bursts, telling us the very latest news, a tempo may be built up in our minds so we expect, even want, information that is swift, short, and immediate. This may make for impatience with research, with historical perspective, with anything in fact that cannot be easily transmitted in short units. Short units do not often lead to a high level of understanding of complex issues. Some issues simply cannot be explained in 30 seconds, not matter how clever the technology. The commercial video medium so far has put an enormously high priority on the swift and the simple. It has little choice, given the existing conditions of competing for eyeball attention, which will wander when the action is not swift and simple.

Perhaps even more significant may be the building up of a common cultural heritage consisting of electronic images. The implications of this are difficult to foresee because we know so little about image memory. If a society shares a cultural heritage that is no longer derived from print, but is derived from current electronic imagery, that image heritage may be devoid of the history of that society, its historical cultural norms, its shared values based on the past. Instead it may be a common cultural heritage of film, TV programs, TV news view of the world, videotapes—all those images stored in memory, "hooked" together heaven only knows how—but acting as the reference guide for values and behavior. (A student reports that families in MacDonalds can be seen acting out the affectionate family behavior shown in MacDonald TV commercials.) No longer can we assume that students share the adults' knowledge of the same written literature or of history. Instead, the young person has stored those images that he or she has actually experienced, which in a 16-year-old means that his or her sense of history may go back only 13 years. The 20-year-old soldier may have an image memory of perhaps 17 years. This may be an inadequate perspective for understanding world issues. But what has happened to what these students read in school or at home? Surely, you say, they read history, and the great literature? They may read some, but not as much as the generation that went to school before World War II, because reading and TV compete with each other. Not only will less information be absorbed from print, but there is the addition of all those images. There is the possibility we mentioned earlier that images, because of their vividness, may be more persistent in memory than words, and so their effect on behavior may be magnified.

If we are moving into a cultural memory bank of images, perhaps we should take very seriously the notion of putting our history as a people onto the imagery medium, requiring that it be viewed by students over and over, like reruns, so that our history becomes part of that memory bank for the generations raised on images.

It is no longer true that the major source of information for children comes from school. At one time in our history, school was where you learned everything you did not learn at home, except for the books you read on your own. Today there are two huge institutions pouring out information to young people—one is the school, but the other is the entertainment industry—TV, film, radio, records, tapes, videotapes. Children today are two channel learners— one channel is what they learn at school, and the other channel is what they learn from the entertainment industry. Will people whose common heritage is recent images behave differently than people who have a common print heritage? Quite possibly. First, the time span of the memory will be much shorter, and therefore there will be a tendency to see issues in the short term. Secondly, images may suggest patterns for behavior that may be more influential than print. Watching images of other young people living well, dancing, partying, engaging in suggestive and unusual sensory experiences, is quite likely to put such patterns of desirable behavior into the heads of peer viewers.

Young adults may develop nostalgia about the past, not meaning the 19th century, but meaning nostalgia over the images they saw when they were younger. Recent successful movies have used this type of nostalgia. The history that is being recaptured is the 1950s, a mere 30 years ago. History, if it is based on electronic images, cannot precede the technology, and that was available only in the 1940s; and history may be restricted to those images one has experienced, which means limiting one's sense of history to one's own lifetime. Anything that happened before one's lifetime is not available information, unless it has been produced and viewed on film or videotape.

Information May Become Redefined as Part of Entertainment.   If information becomes a subjective image, then where will be truth?

The Third Learning Revolution: Speed, Scale, and Imagery.   The first learning revolution, the invention of the alphabet and of writing, was an enormous leap in man's ability to use his mind and his memory. Writing meant that man could go beyond what he could hold in his own short- or long-term memory by using written notes. This made not only records possible, and therefore recorded history, but it meant that man could think about more things than he could hold in his memory. With the aid of written notes, he could organize and plan on a scale not possible if human memory in oral form were his only tool. With writing, he could reflect upon patterns from the past; he could compare one statement to another for analysis; he could utilize written reports about things that he himself had not experienced. He could send messages that would be received in the exact words he had selected. Agreements could be reached that were recorded in the written form to which both parties had agreed, and the contract could be maintained and referred to, in its written state, at any time by either party, rather than relying on human memory for the spoken words.

The second learning revolution, the printing press, multiplied popular access to the written word. If one could read, one had access to whatever was printed. Reading, in itself, is one of the great mind extenders by allowing the reader to go anywhere words will take him or her. Through reading, one can share the experiences of others without having the actual experience. Reading is a great experience-extending tool. Through books, one can extend one's life into other lives, other places, and so develop a taste for something other than one's immediate life and environment. Through reading, one learns religion, history, the literature that is the foundation of a culture—its myths, heros and heroines, martyrs, fairy stories—and one learns of other cultures and of other times.

Perhaps the significance of reading is in its ability not only to bring information to the reader (it is a very efficient database) but to allow the reader to experience vicariously beyond the reach of his or her own life space. Human thought then is able to travel beyond the limits of what one person has experienced, or been told by another person. Reading is an experience magnifier for thinking.

The third learning revolution, which I believe the new information technologies represent, may bring about more radical changes in how we think than either the invention of the alphabet or the invention of type. Not only do these technologies permit us to record data on a scale not possible before, but also to manipulate words and numbers at enormous speed. It is the scale of what is now possible that may force us into new ways of thinking. When we reach the level of 1.5 billion calculations per second, which is 50,000 times faster than the current rate of our personal computers, the human mind is unable to handle that many numbers at that rate. The result has been called *data poisoning,* and those dealing with these calculations in such fields as astronomy have remarked that "no human can assimilate the information in all those numbers. But if you put it in a form of a picture, the human mind can do the ultimate processing" (Robert Duquet programmer, National Radio Astronomy Observatory in Socorro NM, quoted in the Wall Street Journal, 1985). It is quite ironic that imagery will be required to handle the number cruncher!

So one of the changes in human thinking will come about because of the sheer scale and speed of the data a computer can create—so much and so fast that the human mind can not process it as individual pieces of data, but must turn to an image to see the patterns in the data. We had to learn to read so we could comprehend print; now we must learn to "read" images, and to "write" them, if we are to handle this overload of information.

Sometimes still images are not enough. An astrophysicist has reported that individual charts of matter near a black hole were produced by the supercomputer, but not until he animated those computer pictures into a moving film was he able to identify an unusual pattern screen. (Wall Street Journal, 1985). Some information will not be apparent until the images are seen in movement.

My fourth statement was that the technologies should be viewed as the instruments for change that they are, but we as educators should be thinking more about their effects on learning and on society.

And my fifth statement was that education, by which I mean particularly public education, K-12, does not recognize the seriousness of these changes in information and in imagery. If they were taken as seriously as they should be, they would require us to rethink the heart of education itself. Instead, the education establishment is treating the technologies as just another adjunct to the traditional triad of textbook, teacher and test.

There is no denying the power of these visual technologies, power to capture and hold attention. But for what? Will the technologies be put into the service of learning, or will they serve entertainment only?

This is a wide chasm, much wider than seems to be realized. On one side of that chasm we have a huge entertainment industry that takes up a large portion of the average person's day—5 hours or more, according to Neilsen. That is as much time as the average student spends in school each day.

On the other side, we have a huge education industry, which operates in public and private schools, business, and the armed forces.

Education, in its present form, cannot compete with entertainment. Young people's attention is not going to be drawn, spontaneously to talking teachers, to print, to the comparative drabness of the school environment, when they have access to a moving, colorful, quickpaced, even outrageous environment of images. Students will endure the school environment, largely because that is where all the other students are, and some will persist and some will learn a great deal.

But learning, in its traditional form, cannot hold a candle to the pleasures of entertainment in its present form. This is one of the revolutionary conditions of learning today. Learning has stayed in a traditional form, while entertainment has moved into all the dazzling new technologies. So we have a tremendous chasm, which has left the schools almost a century behind—well over a century since the camera was invented (1826); the phonograph record (1877); radio broadcasting more recently (1920); then commercial television (1945); and now microcomputers in 1980. Today, school children learn from film, from records and tapes, from radio, from television, and from computers—the whole range of technologies that are the life blood of the entertainment industry, but that have no central place in public education.

The basic assumption of many schools is that these new technologies should be absorbed into the existing curriculum. I question that assumption. I do not think these technologies are superficial changes that can or should be put into little boxes around the edge of the curriculum.

We must realize that there are many avenues to learning today, not just the classroom. We need to keep pinching our minds so we realize that education comes in many forms, and the students we teach—whether in your schools in your state, or in our classes at Teachers College, all come to class having been educated by many different media before we ever see them as students—and they continue being educated by many different media while we are teaching them. To put this in economic terms, this is a *learner's market.* As educators, we no longer have the exclusive franchise to educate the young. We have instead a lot of competition, most of which is a lot more entertaining than we are.

Even if one could persuade schools that they must change their technology of learning, from print and teacher-talking, to using the entertainment and information technologies to teach, huge problems remain about the cost of conversion, whether it is economically viable, how scholarly learning can be preserved and not sacrificed to entertainment, who will produce the new curriculum, what teachers are prepared to use it, and so on. The redesigning of learning on the new technologies must come, but it will take a long time within the structure called a school, partly because schools do not take easily to changing such fundamental processes, and partly because the staffs in most schools are not trained to use the entertainment and information technologies for learning and teaching.

The redesigning of learning will come, but it may come from the private sector. The computer software industry has had a tough financial struggle trying to sell to the schools and to the home. Videotape may prove more promising, and soon videodisc. But whether the new learning will fit into existing schools is an open question. Perhaps the new learning will require the designing of new schools as well, just as the invention of the printing press helped the development of the common school.

In the new school, the new learning will be at the core of the school's design, not added on to the existing curriculum, and the staff will be prepared to teach and to learn with the new technologies.

The questions for public debate will be: Who will own and run such new schools, answerable to what arm of the public and its government? What our young people are taught, and how, and by whom, responsive to what part of the community, are extremely serious questions.

One of the changes that needs to occur, whether in our traditional school or in a newly designed school, is teaching this generation of young people how to comprehend images, just as once we felt it essential for young people to be taught to read print. If it is true that much, perhaps most, of the information young people are receiving today is coming from electronic images, then they must be taught how to "read" those images. They need to have control over this imagery technology. They need to understand how images are constructed, what the intended effect is on human perception and behavior, the underlying values, the intended and serendipitous messages, and to understand their own reactions to those images. This is an essential part of the appropriate literacy of the late 20th century. Being able to read print is no longer enough, not in a world where most of the information being received is coming via electronic imagery.

POLICY IMPLICATIONS FOR SOCIETY AS A WHOLE

If this quickened tempo of the entertainment and information technologies takes hold, as some claim it has already with our pupil population, then simplistic answers may be increasingly popular at a time when the questions may be more complex. This in turn may lead to support for policies that reduce complex issues to a 2-minute TV news story. The more complex the issue, and the more honestly a public figure may try to present its complexity, the less likely he or she may succeed—unless the public figure can master imagery as a means of communication. The test will be the ability to present matters simply but without distortion, a difficult task.

As computer technology develops into parallel processing, software and hardware may be developed that fit more closely the ways in which the human mind works. This may include simultaneous and more complex patterns of imagery plus words plus music plus speech. This in turn will alter how our information is presented, processed, and acted upon.

In the near future, electronic imagery may change the way in which we define problems and create solutions. As it becomes possible to form images of problems, rather than seeing them spelled out in linear form, we may be able to hold more complex relationships in an image and to see the interactivity of one image with others. If we can do this, we may define problems that are larger in scale, and more interdependent. In turn we may be forced to seek solutions that are longer term, larger in scale, and more sensitive to the interrelationships involved. (This will be in conflict with the quickened tempo and simplistic answers.)

Imagery represents a significant change in our thinking, just as our thinking changed when writing became available. With writing we could have more information available to us, put it in order, lay out steps that required action, and define the elements of a problem. With imagery, we may be venturing into a new way of thinking that is not linear, but perhaps more interdependent.

There is much for concern here, but also much that seems potentially fruitful. The complexity of the issues facing our world certainly require the ability to think broadly, long term, and interrelatedly. Linear solutions to interdependent problems are not likely to work very well, nor have they. Isolating problems for solution is dangerous if the problems, in reality, are not isolated but intertwined. It is possible that imagery thinking may be a critically important tool for looking at a world that has itself become too complex, too intertwined, for linear information to handle or comprehend.

Whether imagery proves to be the fruitful tool we wish, or not, it is certain to become the major information carrier—in fact, it already is. We need to recognize that fact, educate our society to understand imagery as we once taught the reading of print, and begin serious analysis of what it means for a world to learn about itself from images.

WHAT CAN AND SHOULD SCHOOLS DO?

Given a deeper understanding of the learning revolution we are experiencing, what could and should schools do to play a significant and appropriate role?

My first suggestion is that schools choose a role for themselves that is uniquely *educational,* not a role that imitates a corporate office or a factory. Education is a unique institution, with its own history, its own values, its own culture. Schools are not factories. Schools are not—or should not be—imitation corporate offices. Further, I am not persuaded that the American business model, given its recent economic record, is a very sound model for the schools to imitate.

The schools have the chance to change themselves with technology, a chance that I am afraid is being thrown away. Schools could be saying to the nation: "We are going to take the lead in preparing young people for the information age. We are going to use the technologies to their maximum for teaching and learning with all of our students. We are going to educate our young people, not just with technological skills, but with an understanding of how information itself is changing; of how we are moving from print to images;

of what the graphics revolution means for citizenship and occupational roles; of the economic implications of information as a commodity that is being bought, sold and delivered; and what it means in world politics to control the delivery systems of information."

If our schools as a whole take this initiative, and ask for the resources to do the job, I believe the response would be positive.

But instead today I see our schools moving away from the challenge and opportunity that the technologies give us. I see a preoccupation with competency testing, very understandable, but the preoccupation is with print as the way to train for tests, not the technologies. I see textbooks using the technologies as an adjunct to print — a little software to supplement a textbook series, so that the industry commitment is, as it was yesterday, to print, print, print — and I don't hear the schools demanding a better answer. I hear school staff asking for print series that provide coverage of competency test items. The mood today is *curricular alignment.*

What does this trend represent? I think it represents a defensive move to make sure pupils do well on the tests. This is understandable and partially politically useful and necessary. Does it give a leadership role to the schools? No, not if the trend is back to the same curriculum, to the same print textbooks, the same measures of print learning — while our students have become electronic learners; while their parents own and use more technology than the schools; while corporations are racing toward electronic delivery of information. Will our schools be left behind, still teaching through print and speech, while the rest of the world has changed?

If this trend continues, soon we will have no software that does not fit the print textbook formula. Soon we will have no software that encourages a student to explore beyond those curricular gray walls. Soon there will be none of the imagination, the excitement, the discovery, that the best of software brings. We will have thrown away the tools of the information age, in order to defend 19th century print learning.

My final statement was that in my view, the changes we are undergoing are so significant for how we learn, how we remember, and how we form judgments that I think we need to develop a curriculum designed to educate for these changes.

We could be moving into the future, instead of defending the past. What we could be doing is teaching for the Information Age. I am talking about two basic skills of the Information Age that I think are critical.

The first is the skill to evaluate the quality of information. We will be drowning, if we aren't already, in the waves of information coming to us via television, via cable, via computer monitors, via videotape, via videodisc, via communications systems. How much information can one person deal with intelligently? How fast?

We need to teach students how to make these discriminations:

- What is junk information?
- What is quality information in terms of relevance, of accuracy, of dealing with the significance of the information itself?
- When is the most recent information not the best information? There is a terrible tendency with the speedy technologies to think that the most recent is the best. Not necessarily so. How can one tell?
- What is a reliable source of information versus an unreliable one?
- What is a media event, staged for the media, versus a spontaneous newsworthy event?
- How can we tell when video interviews have been skewed to emphasize one point of view?
- How do the technologies themselves, individually, influence and shape the information they carry?
- What are the economic forces that shape information? The statutory and regulatory forces? The political ones?

As you can tell, I am talking about educating students to become intelligent users of information. Much of that information will come in imagery form, which leads me to the second basic skill of the information age.

Among the radical changes being brought by the new technologies is a new language, the language of *imagery*. Imagery is the language of the Information Age. We are learning to conceptualize ideas through imagery; to communicate them through imagery; to develop them through imagery. Imagery has its own attributes, far different than those of print.

We need to teach our students how to understand that imagery. Images are as complex to analyze and to understand as any chapter in any book. Imagery is a new medium that has its own characteristics and, let me add, its own very powerful effects. Images themselves are not new in our history, but their power on film, on tape, on television, on monitors, is a new power.

Images have been developed with enormous impact—to create unthinking admiration for Nazism in Leni Reifenstahl's classic propaganda film, "Triumph of the Will," to persuade all of us to buy products and services in advertising—to develop a particular public personality through public relations—to influence voters through the massive media imagery used in our political elections, to the day-to-day "photo opportunities" of this administration. No one who does not understand imagery can make an informed political judgment. Young people are sophisticated image viewers. This is the stuff of their recreational viewing. But they do not comprehend the power of imagery, how it is created, or how it is designed to influence them. They are not intelligent or, literate, image viewers.

I want young people to be taught what is happening, and happening to them, so they can make informed decisions based on imagery.

These, then, are two of the basic skills for the Information Age. (a) the ability to evaluate the quality of information, and (b) the ability to analyze imagery. I am sure there will be others. What I am suggesting, as strongly as I can, is that we do need to rethink the curriculum because learning itself is changing, because information itself is changing.

Schools need to do this if they are not to lose their role as the prime educator.

If we do not rethink what we are doing, and address these issues our schools could be left behind as education moves out into all those other places that are already changing—and changing a lot more quickly than our schools, into museums, libraries, shopping centers, offices, and along those optical fiber networks into places where we never dreamed education could move.

Our schools—and we as educators—need to finish with the questions of what technology to buy, and where to put it, and to get on with the important educational questions. We need to think carefully about what we need to teach and how we need to teach it for the Information Age. That is an educational question, and about the most important question there is.

We need to concern ourselves with using the technologies to teach all of our children—boys and girls, black and white, Asian and Spanish—so all of them can enter fully into the work of our society. That is an educational question.

We need to put technologies to work in our schools in such a way that we develop humane and caring environments, not male-oriented war-game environments. That is an educational question.

And we need to develop ways to educate our children to understand this Information Age; to evaluate information; and to understand the workings of the enormous power of imagery. All those are educational questions.

What we need to do, then, is to educate as though this technological revolution is what it really is—the third learning revolution—the most important change in learning since the 16th century.

DISCUSSION

Professor Hazel Hertzberg
Teachers College (Social Studies)

I very much welcome Professor White's research. I think it is important. She is asking very important questions. It is, however, at a very early stage. She has not been able to explain to me very clearly some of her ideas on images. It does not mean that they are not important, because when you are on the frontier of thinking, it is not so easy to formulate these ideas. Schools should be pardoned for not immediately changing their curriculum in response to a new perspective that is only beginning and that is not fully developed enough for us to even to have very much of a reaction to it.

Secondly, I suggest that there are some things in White's research that she will look at. It is quite true that print has its own conventions. Of course we know that there are many different kinds of print. There are hieroglyphics for example, there are characters as there are in Chinese and Japanese. There are letters the way we have in English, shaped into words. I do not know whether these various conventions make any difference in learning. I think it's worth checking out rather than simply, without further analysis, lumping all print into one place. Similarly, I very strongly suspect that the electronic media are rather different and I hope that these differences will at least be explored before the idea that they're all the same thing is accepted. Radio, the impact of radio, television, film, and computers—they are all electronic, but it does not seem to me that one learns the same way from all of them. So I hope some more attention will be paid to the different ways that we learn from them.

I wish Professor White luck in her project to put our history as a people into visual form. I do not think it is possible or desirable. I do not want to take that attitude toward print. I'm not willing to accept that we have gone so far along this path that it is impossible for us to use print intelligently and persuasively and as an expansion of the human consciousness. For that reason I am a little taken aback by the characterization of our present time as the age of information. It sounds very good. But there have been many ages of information. I would not think that what started with Guttenberg was not an age of information. So perhaps we need a better term for this particular phenomenon that represents part of our age.

The idea that we are educated by many forces besides the school is actually not a new one. There may be some oldsters in this audience, like myself, who will remember that we have been considering the impact of other agencies that educate students for a great many years, if not centuries. It is not that the other institutions do not change, of course they do, the family, the church, television, and so on. But that is not a recent discovery and it is important to understand that. I would be cautious about such statements as "the home is ahead of the school in terms of the use of electronic media." That implies that this is progress in the home. Maybe it is, but I am not willing to accept that as an assumption without examining it. We should know more than we do now about the impact of computers in the home. We certainly know something about the impact of television in the home and the many prophesies that were made that television would bring the whole family together, staring at the tube. Some of those extravagant claims seem to me to be quite erroneous. So let us be careful about that sort of claim. Just because a great and a powerful new technology is upon us does not mean that our lives have to be completely restructured in order to please it. Human wisdom consists of taking from the past the inherited wisdom of the human race and combining it with whatever it is that we have to cope with in the present, and from this comes a continuing new view of human existence and of education. But I would be rather suspicious of some of the claims of newness. Human beings have coped with technology and the impact of technology for a very long time. I am sure that the discovery of fire was more important. Certainly tools were a more important step in human evolution than the use of the computer. But that doesn't mean that the computer isn't important. But it does mean that we have to look at any new technology in historical perspective, and not simply seek quickly to adjust our whole lives from it without reflection. I know that Professor White was not asking for no reflection. But there is a slight Messianic overtone that she argued about quite a bit that worries me a little. Nevertheless, I think her research is probably the best stuff that's going on right now and is really important. And I'm very glad that she's doing it. I'm just waiting a little cautiously for the results and for the critique of those results.

Professor Willard Jackson,
Teachers College (science education)

Every now and then, but not very often, you read a chapter and say "Gee, I wish I'd said it. How come I didn't think of these things before?" This is one of those chapters. I suggest some of the dangers of not moving in this direction. We need to have our young people developing images that young people in the past have not had. I'd like to do that with a little bit of passion. About 41 years ago, I walked across an open field in the Hartz Mountains. On the field were the bodies of 30 or so German soldiers. I looked at them. They were boys. There wasn't one that was probably over 16 years of age. They were dead. It had begun to smell. It was awful. I think probably the print description of my horrible experience was "American Troops Pushed Another Ten Miles Into The Hartz Mountains Today." Someway or other we have got to convey to our young people the images of warfare and the horror of warfare. I'm all for printed descriptions of it, but I think they are inadequate. I had an experience on the field in the Hartz Mountains that I'm not sure you could convey in print. Some of the new technology may give us a better chance to give our young people to become aware of some of these kinds of experiences, and what may happen if we don't recognize some of these images. So I think the stakes are very, very high.

REFERENCES

Bower, Gordon H. (Ed.) (1983). *The Psychology of Learning and Motivation: Advances in Research and Theory, Vol. 17.* New York: Academic Press.

Kosslyn, S. (1980). *Image and Mind.* Cambridge, Mass.: Harvard University Press.

Paivio, A. (1971). *Imagery and Verbal Processes.* New York: Holt Rinehart & Winston.

Pribram, K. (1985). *APA Monitor,* September 1985, 5–6.

Shepard, R.N. (1978). The mental image. *American Psychologist,* 33 (2), 125–137.

Wall Street Journal, (1985). September 16.

4

Closing the Gap Between Education and Schools

Judah L. Schwartz
*Massachusetts Institute of Technology
and Harvard University*

However we say it, we do not educate our youngsters as well as we would like. The litanies of functional illiteracy abound. The incapacity of the public in the domains of science and mathematics is a national scandal and there is no other industrialized nation that is so oblivious of the languages and cultures of others.

Changing this situation demands a clear vision of what might be and will take commitment at many levels. We are not likely to see that sort of commitment from a mean-spirited administration that has a most simplistic view of intellectuality and its role in our culture. Nor is that administration likely to have a vision of what might be that is any better than a compilation of "what works" as if that were sufficient view of what is worth striving for.

I do not have complete solutions, but I do have a partial vision. I offer it here for discussion in the hope that we may be able to take steps in the direction of that vision before we are reduced to a country whose economy is based entirely on the producing of fast foods and the practicing of litiginous attorneys.

I discuss the role that technology might play in the attainment of this vision. I am aware that technology is but one dimension of the problem. There are, of course, many dimensions to the problem of the reform of education in this country and no approach to the problem along any single one of those dimensions is likely to be sufficient. Nonetheless, it is important to understand the difference between *necessary* and *sufficient.* Insufficient does not imply unnecessary.

In order to help structure the discussion, I respond to a set of questions that was put to me recently by a Task Force of the National Governor's Association concerned with the role of technology in education in the coming decade. These questions are not necessarily framed in ways that I believe to be

67

most appropriate to the issues but they do reflect, in my view, the nature of the present discourse.

QUESTION 1

The first question was: What kinds of training are needed for educators as we move further and further into the information age? The very phrasing of the question betrays a view of the educational enterprise that is inadequate to the information age. To think of the problem of preparing teachers as training implies that the work they are about to undertake is work that requires the mind to function as a muscle. On the other hand, when we think of preparing poets, physicists, painters, philosophers, and pediatricians (i.e., people that must use their minds as minds), we think of education, not training.

How then might the education of educators change to reflect both the demands and the opportunities of the Information Age? I believe that we must educate teachers in the use of the technology to teach subject matter such as science, mathematics, language, history, and literature, as well as educate them to some degree in the technology itself (e.g., programming and the use of generic applications programs such as spreadsheets and databases). We inspect each of these directions in turn.

EDUCATING EDUCATORS TO USE TECHNOLOGY TO TEACH SCIENCE, MATHEMATICS, LANGUAGE, HISTORY, AND LITERATURE

For the most part, teachers, particularly at the elementary level, are not well enough educated in these subject areas. We have always assumed that teaching those skills necessary for functioning in the society does not require any deep understanding of the intellectual disciplines from which those skills are derived. It has become increasingly clear in recent years that this is a serious error of judgment. If a teacher is to be sensitive and responsive to a youngster's idiosyncratic formulation of a problem then he or she must have a sense of the larger intellectual landscape and where within it the child's formulation fits.

Most teachers do not regard themselves as continuing learners of the subjects they teach their students. One of the distinguishing characteristics of a great university is that the faculty regard themselves, and are regarded by the students, as a community of scholars. If the object of education is to have students come to understand that they should regard themselves as lifelong learners then perhaps they should see their teachers as lifelong learners.

Carefully crafted software, that draws on what we are learning about the nature of human cognition, can enable learners (be they students or teachers) to explore their own growing understanding. A good piece of software is one that is about a set of ideas and not about a piece of curricular content at some grade level or a part of a scope and sequence. For Example, the GEOMETRIC SUPPOSER is about the mathematics of shape in the Euclidean plane and has been used richly and productively in middle school and at university. It is an environment in which a learner (who might be a teacher) can explore his or her own conjectures about a range of possible relationships among shapes. When students devise new mathematical theorems and spontaneously discover the need for formal mathematical proof, then something different is happening in the mathematics classroom.

Similarly, when in the context of SIR ISAAC NEWTON'S GAMES, a 7-year-old can devise an explanation of centripetal acceleration based on an understanding of the composition of vectors, then something different is happening in the science classroom.

Getting deep insight into important ideas does not only happen in science and mathematics software environments. M-SS-NG L-NKS and WORD QUEST provide software environments in which the tacit knowledge of a user of a language (be it English, French, Spanish, or German) can explore his or her own understanding of a rich set of issues ranging from phonetics to word structure to literary style.

In a community of learners, intellectual authority derives from evidence and argument and not from assertion. The price one pays for this sort of vigorous community of learners is one that may not be comfortable. If people approach the task of teaching youngsters in the expectation that the setting is one in which their authority will be unquestioned then they will not be comfortable in the world of schools that I am envisioning. On the other hand, if they are attracted to the challenge of helping people to think originally and critically about themselves and their world than they will be comfortable. Perhaps we will see new sorts of teachers and teaching.

In addition to educating educators to learn and teach the subject areas with technology (as well as other tools), we must educate them in the technology itself (e.g., in the use of programming languages and generic applications programs such as databases and spreadsheets. There are however, serious difficulties that stand in the way of doing that. To begin with we must recognize that a programming language, databases, spreadsheets, and text editors are problem-solving tools. In order to use them, one must have a problem that one wants to solve. Problems of interest and import derive from the subject areas. The competent use of what appear to be specifically technological tools depends on a user having an inquiring mind eager to solve problems. Thus we see that the resolution of the problem of educating educators in the technology is not independent of the problem of educating educators in the subject areas.

Over and above those difficulties, there are some difficulties that derive from the very nature of these technological tools. Let us consider some of them.

Programming

People by nature do not seem to think procedurally. There would seem to be little point in continuing the present practice of using teachers who are themselves rather poor programmers to teach youngsters to be even poorer programmers, when in fact almost the uses of computers that any of us make call for the use of generic applications programs. At present, where programming is part of the curriculum, it is usually justified as being a sort of new Latin (i.e., the subject one studies in order to learn to think more clearly). That may well be true someday, when the overhead of specific syntactic requirements and forms of control structures of particular languages are no longer mistaken for "laws of thought." The present situation can be likened to those who think the playing of scales is the making of music. This is another illustration of the price of confusing necessary with sufficient.

Databases

Boolean connectives are seemingly not understood. In general the competent use of databases requires a careful, rather than a sloppy understanding of the words "and," "or," and "not." I have watched youngsters not understand why a database on United States presidents, when queried about the number of presidents born in Massachusetts and Vermont, insisted on claiming that no presidents were born in Massachusetts and Vermont. Clearly, the problem has nothing to do with the technology. Rather we need to educate people to use the language with much greater precision than they are presently accustomed to using.

Spreadsheets

Recently, an article in a major newspaper estimated that over 40% of the spreadsheets in use in the country today contain errors that derive from the referents of quantity not being used properly (e.g., adding months to dollars and subtracting square feet). All quantity that we use in modeling the world about us is adjectival in nature (i.e., it has referents). Not taking these referents into account leads to analytic barbarism. Again the resolution of the problem is not a problem in the use of the technological tool called *spreadsheet*. The problem lies in the fact that we teach mathematics as if numbers were nouns. A proper restructuring of the mathematics curriculum that takes into account the referential nature of the quantities used in modeling has already been shown to helpful on this score.

Text Editors

Text editors by themselves do not repair grammar or clarify thought. A teacher who does not write well and regularly can hardly be expected to teach someone else to do so. Once again the solution to the problem of the effective use of the technological tool lies in the broader and deeper and more challenging education of educators in the subject areas.

QUESTION 2

The second question the Governor's Task Force asked me to think about was: What kinds of action are necessary to redress inequities in technology rich educational settings?

In my view, it is important to distinguish inequities of access and inequities of expectation. To be sure, inequities of access are important. But there indications that these problems are being solved. Moreover, it is also clear that resolving problems of inequities of access, does not by itself resolve problems of a far more insidious sort of inequity (i.e., the inequity of expectation).

Even where technology is being introduced to communities that have traditionally not been well served by the educational system, it is often the case that the effort is driven by the fashionable nature of the innovation and without adequate regard for the broader school context.

Specifically, I believe that resource inequities must be addressed in an appropriate sequence, to wit;

- Children must have love and food before school is likely to matter much to them.
- Schools must have textbooks and libraries before they can be expected to attract caring and demanding teachers.
- Caring and demanding teachers must think of themselves as, and must be, continually learning intellectuals and professionals before they are able to take advantage of, with confidence and competence, the products of new technologies.

It is only those teachers who are confident and competent that can look to each and every child and expect excellence. In my view, we will not resolve the most serious equity problem of all (i.e., the problem of the inequity of expectation without a new vision of the teacher as a continuing learner who respects and treasures the diversity of the students that he or she teaches).

QUESTION 3

Finally, the third question the Governor's Task Force asked me to consider was: What kinds of changes must schools undergo in order that they may use technology to be more productive?

Answering this question depends on a working definition of productivity. Jonathan Swift had an irreverent view of those who pressed for an immediate and pragmatic utility for all human undertaking when he asked, "And of what use, Sir, is a baby?" Our overwhelming national temptation is to measure productivity in measures that have short time constants. We do this in business and have produced a generation of business-school executives who can run anything but can make nothing as they chase the next quarter's Return On Investment figures. We also do this in education, where we press our teachers to teach and test that which can be simple mindedly tested. In the end we mistake excellence in education for a larger fraction of our students who can pass minimal competence examinations. Our society, and indeed, the human species requires that we have a longer view and a more thoughtful view of productivity as well.

Roughly speaking, we can map short time productivity of education onto the ability of every person coming out of the schools to find gainful employment, and long-term productivity of education onto the ability of every person to realize some substantial fraction of the promise and potential that he or she has to lead an interesting life and to contribute to the happiness and well-being of others.

Clearly, we must all make some judgment of appropriate balance between these long- and short-term definitions of productivity. I have tried to argue that for the most part the judgments we now make are lop-sided in favor of the short term. Others may argue, that the judgments they make are reasonable in the face of the real demands and resources of the society. But if anything is true about an emerging Information Age, it is that the demands and the resources of the society will shift. What follows is a scenario of technological development that is likely to cause each of us to reinspect his or her prior judgment.

Within a small number of years the technology of broadcast television will change dramatically by virtue of the introduction of digital television (i.e., the processing of signals in the home television receiver by digital rather than analog circuitry).

The computational power of the digital home television receiver and its associated interface devices (keyboard and mass storage such as videocassette recorder, VCR) will be dramatically greater than the more powerful of todays personal computers.

These TV receivers will be very widespread because the market driving their distribution is fundamentally a home entertainment market rather than a business or education market.

Because the cost of distributing "educational" and other software to the home will be low, there is likely to arise a new sort of educational mechanism in the society, one that uses this medium to train children at home in isolation in the skills that can more or less be learned in isolation. These skills are for the most part the skills that constitute by far the largest part of the present school curriculum. They are such things as learning to read and simple number facts and computation. Educational television has already demonstrated its ability to do this sort of thing very well, even without the high degree of interactivity that the medium will soon possess. There is every reason to believe that the future broadcast medium can do even better in "delivering" this sort of education.

If the school's current instructional agenda is taken over by this new medium, what will schools do? I believe that schools will continue to exist but if they are to do so with more than a simply custodial function, they must be willing to do something beyond what they now think of as their major responsibility (i.e., the teaching of reading, writing, and arithmetic). They must become centers for the learning and teaching of that which cannot be learned and taught in isolation.

CONCLUSION

Formulating and solving problems are not solitary acts. In fact, I believe that problem solving is a paradigmatic human social activity. The thoughtful and creative use of the new technologies has shown us that we can expand and enhance people's abilities to formulate and solve problems. Let these new educational channels in the society train youngsters in the necessary, but totally insufficient, sets of skills that schools now focus their attention on, and let the schools of the country seize the intellectual high ground. Only in that way can we become the free, caring, and learning society we should be.

DISCUSSION

Lucy Calkins' Response to Judah Schwartz' Remarks

Judah began, I think, very appropriately, talking about the importance of having a vision of what might be. It seems that everybody these days is talking about the importance of having a vision. Boyer has talked a lot about how one of the problems in schools, however, is that goals tend to proliferate like barnacles on the hull of a weathered ship. The problem with having so many goals is that we don't hold ourselves accountable for any of them. My fear is that after listening to Judah, we will return to our school districts with fifteen new goals, and that we won't be able to implement them. We need to sift through all the different things that Judah has said and try to identify what really is our priority. What is the main message?

For me, the main message comes down to the importance of teachers, to the importance of educating teachers. Certainly it is true that what happens in schools is filtered through the hearts and minds of teachers. We heard a lot about how important it is that there be a community of learners in classrooms and that the teacher be a member of that community; that in classrooms there be collaborative learning, where people are interacting; that teachers learn to be comfortable teaching at the frontier. There has been talk of the importance of moving from the gasoline pump model to the apprenticeship model in our classrooms.

The point I want to raise is that all of these important things challenge the givens of our classrooms. We know from John Goodlad's study that American classrooms are characterized by passivity, by teachers doing most of the talking, by a gasoline pump model of education. What we are talking about here is finding a way to change the givens of classrooms, to change what classrooms look and sound and feel like.

These givens have characterized schools for generations. Over the years, there have been, and will be, radical new methods in agriculture, in accounting, in medicine. But in education, the way my great-grandmother was taught is very much the way my child will be taught. The givens persist.

When we talk about technology in the classrooms, we are talking about trying to help educators form radically new images of what classrooms should look, sound, and feel like. If that is going to happen, we as supporters of teachers, as leaders of teachers, as educators of teachers, need to have new givens to characterize our staff development. How often do we really, ourselves, model what it is to be powerful learners in a school building? We have to create occasions for learning in school buildings. We have to encourage teachers to spend time reading and meeting with each other and learning collaboratively. Seymour Sarason said the notion that teachers can create conditions that are stimulating and alive for children, when those same conditions do not exist for teachers, has no warrant in the history of mankind.

I want to make a plea for us to take the responsibility on our shoulders. Instead of pointing to teachers and saying teachers should do this and teachers should do that, we need to ask what *we* can do. Perhaps the most important thing for us to think about is the role we can play in making schools places for professional learning.

Professor Bruce Vogeli, Mathematics

There are so many appealing ideas and appealing phrases in this presentation that it is difficult to pick out those that can be responded to adequately in a few minutes: "a vigorous community of scholars," "Ideas not technology," "Caring and demonstrative," "Confident and competent teachers," and "carefully crafted software." Each of these deserve a response and I unfortunately will not be able to give it. I'd like to concentrate on the ideas, not technology principle.

Clearly the failure of software in the area of mathematics to produce significantly enhanced learning is due not to the technology, but to the ideas that are being implemented, or that are attempting to be implemented, through the technology. I would challenge Professor Schwartz. I don't think we know how to teach problem solving, with human teachers or electronic teachers. Until we do, that carefully crafted software is not the answer to enhancing student's problem solving ability. I do not believe that media, television, Children's Television Workshop, or other mass communication efforts in the area of mathematics have been successful. I've recently previewed a new series on mathematics, a major effort by the Children's Television Workshop, and found it sorely wanting, both in pedagogical skill and mathematical content. I am not sure that technology in the absence of a wealth of ideas concerning the teaching of mathematics and science is the answer. I agree with Professor Calkins and with Professor Schwartz that a confident and competent teacher is an essential ingredient in the educational process. But I believe that carefully crafted software will not emerge in sufficient quantities to improve significantly the teaching of science and mathematics in this century until there is a richer storehouse of ideas supported by educational research that will allow us to carefully craft the software that Professor Schwartz anticipates.

Curriculum for the Information Age: An Interim Proposal

Julie McGee
Ligature, Inc.

About 6 years ago, the personal computer began to appear in large numbers in secondary schools throughout the country. In those heady days, the computer evangelists among us believed that the computer would radically alter the face of education, that it could make individualized learning truly possible, that it could motivate children and tie their education to the "real world." All those hopes, although grand, were legitimate possibilities; and they still are just that—possibilities. What we did not count on was the rigidity of the curriculum, the resistance or disinterest of teachers and administrators, the shifting sands of educational priorities, and the fundamental lack of focus that confronts both our schools and our society.

What is happening in classrooms today is the subjugation of the technology to the conventional: the breath of fresh air that technology seemed to promise is going into familiar bottles with the same old labels. An examination of the impact of technology on the language arts area can reasonably represent what has occurred in the other academic disciplines. The English teacher who studied when I did probably loves literature and books and wants to share that love with students. Quite sincerely, this teacher may believe that responding to technology will necessarily take something vital out of the curriculum, a learning activity that has enriched students' lives. An energetic, imaginative English teacher told me several years ago, "I wouldn't mind using computers, but how can I fit it in? There just isn't enough time." The key words here are "wouldn't mind"; responding to and using the technology simply is not a priority. Continuing the present curriculum is. This response typifies the attitude of many fine, responsible teachers. My son, a freshman at a prestigious suburban high school with a student-to-computer ratio of 10 to 1, has not used a computer once this school year. Yet, his teachers are regarded as among the best in the school.

In some schools, the answer to technology has been to fit the computer into the existing curriculum. The question then becomes not what new experiences the technology might provide, but how to use it to support traditional learning activities. In the English classroom, fitting the technology to the traditional curriculum has meant teaching word processing as an adjunct to the teaching of composition. An examination of computer-related activities at the National Council of Teachers of English (NCTE) is instructive in this regard. In 1981 I became a member of a new committee, the Standing Committee on Instructional Technology. We thought of ourselves as a pioneering group that wanted to see the computer become part of the mainstream English teaching process. We planned seminars on the different kinds of software and explored the merits (or lack of them) in drill-and-practice, tutorials, and simulations. We presented programs on selecting software, tried to inspire teachers to use the software, and planned computer configurations within schools. We were the Pied Pipers, leading the masses to a brave new, computing world. At the NCTE annual convention, computer sessions were especially well attended, and our enthusiasm soared.

Then an interesting thing happened to me; I was invited to join the NCTE Commission on Media, a group comprised of people with interests in film, television, photography, and, yes, computers. I began to see that in the eyes of the mainstream teaching profession, the computer was becoming the latter day television or film, an interesting adjunct to education but not an essential part of it. The NCTE convention programs themselves reflect this bias. Media-related sessions (including computers) have held less that 10% of program slots for the last 10 years. The traditional learning activities of composition, literature, language, and reading, still control the program. The lack of a visible computer presence on the program is an accurate reflection of what is happening in English classrooms today. If anything, the convention program is likely to be a little ahead of the curriculum in the average school. There is one notable exception to this trend: Each year more and more sessions are available on using word processing to facilitate the teaching of composition. Most English teachers seem to agree that word processing is the most appropriate adaptation of the technology to the curriculum. They certainly do not expect to see the curriculum adapt to the technology or to its impact on society.

The English teacher's response to technology is not an isolated occurrence. The standardization of computer applications across the curriculum in the average school presents the real danger that using technology will become the province only of the teacher particularly dedicated to its use. The fact that students may enjoy these teachers' classes more will serve only to reinforce the general suspicion that there is something a little peculiar about people who use computers or any other technology. These attitudes are not likely to change as long as the curriculum remains locked in tight boxes labeled history, math, science, English, and so on.

This series of difficulties is compounded by the resistence or disinterest of many teachers and administrators toward technology in the classroom. Too many schools place the highest value on the most traditional form of education; the teacher talks, the students listen and occasionally respond, preferably in writing. This bias is often reflected in the teacher-evaluation process. An administrator who arrives for his or her yearly visit on a day when non-traditional activities are taking place is likely to tell the teacher, "I'll come back on a day when you're teaching." (Translation: talking while students listen.) This administrator does not know how to evaluate the teacher in the role of collaborator in the learning process instead of dispenser of knowledge. The administrator can make his or her preference for standardized classrooms evident in other ways as well. One especially effective way to stifle the use of technology is to make it inaccessible in the practical sense. In some schools, teachers must order films a year in advance and hope that their classes are at the right point in the curriculum on the chosen day. A classroom full of computers with a key kept far away and software available in still another location is not going to draw teachers as readily as one that is accessible and easy to utilize. Even better, teachers need access to the technology in their own classrooms. A school system that does not actively value the use of technology as reflected in evaluation procedures and peer recognition is not encouraging its use. Is it any wonder that teachers working in such systems find it more comfortable to stick with the "tried and true"? Unfortunately, much of the tried and true is close to becoming tired and false because it is out of touch with the real world in which the students must live.

Still, the administrator and teacher alike are victims of constantly changing educational priorities, shifting agendas that grab headlines, parental interest, and governmental actions today that are often ignored tomorrow. One might argue that these changes reflect growth and advancement in the educational process; a more cynical view is that many educational priorities are merely fads, much as our teenagers may sport spiked hair today and velvet tomorrow. Only a few years ago, technology was gaining substantial public attention, both in the press and in school board meetings. No one wanted to be left out of the advancing technological future, and schools hastened to buy computers, often without knowing how to use them in a productive manner. It should come as no surprise then that some disillusionment inevitably followed or that in many schools today a limited number of teachers make use of the technology on a regular basis.

What progress in the use of technology should we expect in the next few years? The priorities of state legislators, currently the primary impetus for educational change, as reported in *Education USA* (Jan. 13, 1986) are funding, teacher education, and testing. Thirty-six states report that financing education is their top concern this year. The effect of federal budget cuts will be to force states to search out every available source of revenue to make up for lost federal dollars. The traditional avenues for raising money for education, raising the income tax and the property tax, are probably not acceptable alternatives in most states. Voters have repeatedly shown their reluctance to pay more money for better schools. Improving the quality of education costs money. Certainly, the successful, widespread use of technology in the curriculum will be expensive.

Another aspect of the concern about money is the relatively low level of teacher compensation. One survey after another shows that teacher pay continues to lag behind that of other professions, averaging about $25,000 a year nationwide. Many talented undergraduates today who could be the top teachers tomorrow will not be attracted to a profession so low in pay. However, the concern over teacher pay may mask the genuine problem. It may be a symptom, not the disease itself. If teachers had real prestige in the eyes of their communities, then adequate salaries would follow. How to restore prestige to teachers in the context of education today is an issue few are willing to address. Yet we expect teachers to work overtime to incorporate new technologies into the curriculum when they face larger class loads due to the continuing funding crisis and scarcely visible public support in terms of pay and prestige.

Instead of support, teachers are finding that they are under siege, forced in many states to take humiliating competency exams to ensure their continued employment. Even though the vast majority pass these tests with ease, many feel that the process itself calls their professionalism into open question. The emphasis in much of the current attention to education, the fads of the moment, if you will, misses the real point of assuring that students are getting a full education that will enrich their lives.

Instead, students, like teachers, are taking minimum competency examinations; the name says all that is necessary. When schools must teach for minimum competencies, then students are trained, not educated. They are trained to answer questions, to pass tests—not to think, not to solve problems, not to delight in learning.

This troubled environment is the real world in education today. It is a world that lacks a clear focus, a world that measures, instead of exciting students and teachers alike. It is a world not unlike the larger society of which it is a part. Sociologist David Riesman says, "Everyone is unsettled. It adds to the sense of turmoil, bewilderment, in which we all live." (*US News,* March 24, 1986) Rudolph Weingartner, Dean of the College of Arts and Sciences at Northwestern University, warns, "Deep conflict about ends, about goals, about outcomes of life" persists because the U.S. lacks "underlying social and cultural coherence." (*Chronical of Higher Education,* Jan. 22, 1986).

In this environment, significant change to accomodate technology in the curriculum is unlikely to occur. What is needed instead is an available, if less than radical, solution—an interim solution that addresses the needs of students and respects the realities confronting teachers and schools today.

The Information Age has thrust upon us, students and educational leaders and soothsayers alike, complexities that did not exist 30 years ago. When my generation graduated from college, the consensus was that we had three fundamental decisions to make: what profession to follow, which company to work for, and whom to marry. We fervently believed that these choices, once made, were made for life. One has only to look at any statistical study of American life to see that most of us re-make some of these decisions many times.

Social critic Alvin Toffler, one of the first to bring popular attention to the accelerated pace of change in our society, reflected recently on the "explosion of choice" we confront. No longer do we have only the three clearly defined choices of job, employer, and spouse. We have to know which college our children should attend, which new car to buy, how to choose an IRA, how to dress for success, how to do a power lunch as we move up the corporate ladder, how to find the perfect mate, and so on. In fact, an entire bookstore in Philadelphia is devoted to "how to" books: a perfect symbol for an insecure age.

Is the advent of technology responsible for the changes we see around us? To some extent, yes. Today change occurs at such a pace that people must seek new training repeatedly in order to remain employable or to be effective in their work. The family doctor (who probably no longer exists except in memory) now confronts more change in 10 years than formerly occurred in 100. An engineer who studied 30 years ago finds his training largely eclipsed by a technology that can do the same work in a fraction of the time. A pilot who learned to calculate weight-balance formulae by hand can now buy a small, navigational calculator to accomplish the same task more accurately in less time. The professions for which we trained have been profoundly altered by the influx of technology. Consequently, our fundamental attitude toward education must change—to education as a lifelong activity.

I was educated to be a teacher of English. That meant I read great literature and took a single methods course. I remember a few educational psychology courses, requirements my classmates universally disdained as odious and irrelevant. As I looked toward the future 25 years ago, I expected to take more courses in literature, which is exactly what I did, including 15 graduate hours in Milton. If Milton did succeed in justifying "the ways of God to man," I was never able to justify to any high-school student a good reason for following in my footsteps. It reminds me of the tired joke about the meaning of BS, MS, and Ph.D. But there is truth in the fact that we did learn "more of the same." Today's students cannot afford that luxury. Indeed, as I look back, it seems a luxury that I could explore the images of *Samson Agonistes* and the philosophical basis of the *Aeropagitica,* something today's student is probably too practical to do. Today's young person looks toward a future far less certain than ours seemed to be, a future where the only certainty is change, where the only pathway to success is to be prepared to rethink our education and seek more, to reorder our priorities, to make accurate decisions, to use information intelligently, and somewhere along the way, we hope, to retain a careful respect for the quality of human life in this world.

The problem is not the technology itself. Technology is, in fact, advancing faster than our ability to cope with it. The problem is that we must assess and respond to technology's impact on our lives. And the answer requires a definition of skills, abilities, and attitudes that we want students to acquire.

REORDERING THE CURRICULUM

I propose that we need to reorder the curriculum to emphasize a new hierarchy of skills, skills that will equip students for life in the Information Age. The skills that we need are (a) the ability to evaluate information, (b) the ability to set priorities, and (c) the ability to make decisions.

The classroom teacher has at his or her fingertips the tools to teach these skills and to teach them within a philosophic framework that creates responsible human beings.

The Ability to Evaluate Information

The proliferation of information creates problems that schools must address. Do students know the difference between a primary and a secondary source? With the many sources of information flooding over us, how do we know which ones are valid and which are not? Let us look at some sample learning experiences and examine how the evaluation of information can be presented.

Lesson One: An elementary-school student has to prepare a report on George Washington. The student pulls out an encyclopedia, summarizes the article in a page, and turns it in. The students get a grade. End of lesson—end of learning. Let's take a different approach. How could a teacher turn this exercise into a learning experience about both George Washington and information? One way would be to compare articles from several encyclopedias. What points does each stress? Does one contain facts that the others do not? The teacher could copy a page from a history book on the American Revolution, and the students could compare that information with the information in the encyclopedia. If the class has access to an on-line computer, an article from the electronic encyclopedia could be an interesting counterpart to the printed one. At the end of our revised lesson, the student would have acquired valuable tools for evaluating information, and the teacher could lead students into seeing the value of examining multiple sources of information and of knowing where to look for particular kinds of information. Importantly, students could begin to see that how information is organized can affect how it is perceived.

Lesson Two: Two debate teams have carefully prepared notes, hundreds of notecards in fact, for a debate on nuclear power. As the last speaker finishes his summation, he quotes from what he believes to be an authoritative source—the *Reader's Digest.* Aghast, the judge awards the match to the opposing team. The debate coach failed utterly to teach his students, who had invested many hours and much energy, that one source of information is not necessarily as good as another.

Lesson Three: A high school student has to prepare an argumentative essay on a topic of his own choosing; unfortunately, that topic is likely to be a popular but overused one like abortion, the legalization of marijuana or capital punishment. Instead of the usual trip to the library and excursion through the pages of the *Reader's Guide to Periodical Literature,* the teacher could give a sample lesson on evaluating information. An article on nuclear power plants from a publication supported by Lyndon LaRouche could be contrasted with one from an anti-nuclear group. Both articles would purport to present information, but a skilled teacher can help students to detect bias. This analysis could occur in a social studies class or even a math class. (The misuse of statistical evidence is one of the primary tasks faced in evaluating information, yet rarely are students taught how to analyze charts and numbers.) This lesson also points to the need for cross-disciplinary work in teaching, for teaching across the curriculum. As long as we remain in our carefully constructed curricular divisions, students cannot gain the benefit of integrating information.

All along the line, we do not teach how to evaluate information. It can be done. Significantly, it can be done within the existing curricular framework. What is required is that the teacher make it a priority. I argue that it is a critical priority. It also happens to be one in which the technology can be utilized effectively.

For example, a school with access to a large database through an on-line computer could show children how to use the computer to find out what they need to know; how to ask questions that will elicit from the database the required information; how to evaluate that information once received. One very real danger is that people often assume that information received through a computer terminal is somehow more accurate than that heard on television or read in print. Marketing organizations are already using that prejudice to entice consumers into purchases on-line. I was present in a meeting when a marketing manager said, "Let's program the computer to tell the consumer what to buy.

They'll be more likely to take that as objective information than something the salesman tells them." In fact, studies bear out his contention.

Looking for information can be an exciting game, a detective story for the mind. A geneologist looks for information about the past and often must search through many sources to unravel the history of a family. A reporter can be a detective of the present by examining public records to uncover corruption or reveal problems that require attention. Teachers who draw attention to the excitement of discovery that information can provide in any discipline are helping create the inquisitive student whose life is enriched by his education.

The Ability to Set Priorities

Setting priorities is a life skill to which schools pay scant attention. Adults assume that students understand priorities and somehow expect that those priorities will match their own. Invariably, that expectation meets with disappointment. On some occasions, adults fail to understand a young person's culture that values skateboards over books, or fast cars over solving algebraic equations. Unfortunately, many young people today lack the simple tools to analyze their situations and set meaningful priorities. Because many people learn from the examples of their parents and peers how to set priorities, those who lack appropriate role models may not have adequate information about this important life skill. However, the schools are in the position to help students understand priorities and their meaning.

A person must deal with two types of priorities: *life priorities,* which are the larger values and goals that provide direction in life; and *short-term priorities,* which are more immediate and which can be satisfied through specific actions or accomplishments. Life priorities tend to be established by family, religion, and culture at an early age. These priorities tend to remain constant even though the emphasis at some particular point may shift, or the priorities themselves change. The social studies provides an effective arena for the examination of both life and short-term priorities. Abraham Lincoln, for example, had certain life priorities, the value of education being one, that shaped his life. He also had short-term priorities in terms of his political career and his goals once elected to the office of President. Literature, likewise, has many examples of characters whose priorities either exalted their lives or brought them grief. King Lear's need to affirm his daughters' love for him caused his priority to change; he abandoned his duty (his life priority) to rule, and it brought tragedy both to him and to his kingdom.

This skill is one that the people of the Information Age especially need to understand. Just as education must become a lifelong activity, the underlying understanding of the priorities that shape our choices and decisions and give structure and meaning to our lives becomes even more vital than ever. Priorities may, in fact, need to be adjusted many times in the course of one's career, academic and otherwise. What is needed is a structure that makes understanding this process possible.

A useful structure for analyzing priorities is to ask a series of questions about one's goals.

1. Is this goal achievable? Is it vulnerable to change? Part of the American ethic is the belief that anything is possible, that a poor boy (dare we hope girl?) may aspire to be President.

   a. Do I have the knowledge to achieve this? If not, can I get it?

   b. Do I have the skills to reach this goal? Can I acquire them?

   c. Do I have the resources in terms of time, money, physical stamina, etc.? If not, are they available to me?

2. Finally, how willing am I to invest myself in achieving this goal?

This process will work for analyzing priorities as simple as a desire for a more physically fit body to the more complex and psychological goal of a career in medicine or a happy marriage. This structure is effective in analyzing business decisions or life decisions and can easily become part of the educational process. It is, in the popular educational jargon of today, a problem solving skill, and it is one that can be taught.

The Ability to Make Decisions

Making decisions seems, on the surface, a simple matter: to go or not to go; to read this book or not; to buy this pair of shoes or not. And it is true that once a person has evaluated information effectively and set clear priorities for him or herself, the decisions will naturally enough flow from those actions. Educators can assist students in making effective decisions by teaching process; understanding process is the additional survival skill that we required in the Information Age.

When computers first came on the educational scene, some large claims about how using them appropriately would develop problem solving skills were made by everyone from Seymour Papert to the U.S. Department of Education. Little empirical evidence exists that learning Logo will give a young person an ability to apply problem-solving skills in other areas of life. For example, the analysis of geometric proofs is a supremely logical activity; yet we all know mathematicians who cannot make simple decisions about life and apply their so-called problem-solving skills to everyday matters. It is also true that schools have routinely robbed students of the right to make decisions about their education and their lives, but the answer to that circumstance may not be the technology itself. The technology makes it more urgent, however, that an answer be found.

Educators increasingly are addressing the need to teach process in all areas of the curriculum. Meta-cognition, the process of learning, is gaining attention in the development of texts and teaching strategies. Much research in writing today, for example, centers on the process of writing. How do we get from an idea to a finished product? What processes do we need to understand in order to write? John Henry Martin's program, developed with IBM, "Writing to Read," is an example of a project that emphasizes the process of writing by incorporating instruction in writing with instruction in reading. Using the computer, cassette tapes, and typewriters, students in kindergarten are writing stories, good stories, fun stories, stories that give them a sense of achievement about themselves and their abilities. The evidence that this program works does exist. An extensive testing program, conducted by the Educational Testing Service (ETS), confirms that students are indeed learning to read and write using "Writing to Read." Other significant research in how to teach writing includes the various Writing Projects that have developed from the results of an early one in the Bay Area of San Francisco.

An example of how a gifted teacher presented a routine writing assignment to a class of fifth graders may be instructive. She asked students to write a paper about their summer vacation—that most vapid of assignments, one that any of us who ever received it, recall with some horror. But then she gave her students the tools to write the paper by taking them into the process. After the groans subsided, she asked everyone to take out a sheet of paper and write the alphabet in a column down the lefthand side of the page. Then she said, "Write something you did this summer that starts with an "A." Soon, the list was growing, and children were asking, "Can I put down more than one thing for some letters?" The teacher was giving the children the tools to discover that their lives had been more interesting than they, at first, thought. She also created excitement and enthusiasm about what could have been the most routine of assignments. The list completed, the teacher led her students through the process of deciding which of all these things they should write about. She did not want a list of activities for a paper—not "I dug up an Ant hill; I rode my Bicycle; I baked a Cake; I Decorated for a party," etc. She helped students to see which of their experiences were rich in the detail that makes for interesting writing. Then, she wrote the assignment with her students, and they shared their experiences by reading the papers to one another. Because the teacher shared the process of writing with her students, she helped them understand the concrete process of finding an idea and deciding what to do.

Schools also should be actively engaged in teaching the process of thinking, especially problem-solving and critical-thinking skills. Although much has been written about these skills as appropriate educational goals, it seems unlikely that much of that theory is being transfered to the average classroom today. Because teachers themselves have little decision-making power over their own jobs and how they are organized, it should not be surprising that they have difficulty teaching students how to exercise or develop these skills as well.

Teaching process can also involve teaching how we decide—the process of decision making. Many decisions that we make never go through a formal, conscious process. Some decisions are intuitive and simply evolve over a period of time. But schools can teach methods of decision making. One model of decision making can be described as hierarchical. In this process, a person proceeds from Point A and its accompanying decision to Point B and its decision, and so on. The components of an issue are divided into sequential, organized steps, and this process follows a step-by-step procedure. Another process is more relational than sequential. In this model, which can be meta-phorically described as *global* instead of *linear,* a person deals with the multiple aspects of a decision simultaneously. It is important that we understand how we decide so that the process can be used to our benefit.

Literature is replete with examples of decisions made and not made and of the consequences of these choices. For this reason, the study of literature can provide an environment for examining the decision-making process. In fact, almost all literature turns on the dynamics of setting priorities and making decisions. In *The Scarlet Letter,* the minister Dimmesdale first decided to hide his sin and then later to expose it in order to win salvation. Huck Finn decided not to turn the runaway slave Jim in to the authorities. Hamlet decided to revenge his father's death and kill his uncle. But in Hamlet's words, "There's the rub." Decisions without actions, without consequences, lack validity. Ham-let made a decision but failed to act and was, as a result, doomed. On the other hand, Thoreau, Martin Luther King, and Gandhi acted on their decisions and changed history.

How do we transfer this process to our students and to ordinary human beings? That, of course, is more difficult. Literature and history are "real," but they are not the same as the students' lives. It would be tempting to say that computer-based simulations could give children the opportunity to make deci-sions within a controlled environment. Oregon Trail, one of the first widely used computer-based simulations, won much praise for that reason. Other exciting simulations followed. Still, there is no reason to suppose that making decisions in a computer environment is a process that readily transfers to students' lives.

When I began this speech, I believed I would make a modest proposal for change in how we educate our children, a proposal that could be implemented within the existing curricular framework. I believed that such a proposal would have a greater chance of success, given the realities of education.

What I have proposed suggests that we must fundamentally rethink how we educate our children, what our priorities are, and how we think and make decisions.

Samuel Goldwyn said, "Never make predictions, especially about the future." Nonetheless, I make a prediction or two about the likelihood that this proposal or any of the others in this book are implemented in the near future. The prognosis is grim. The structure of organizing education has not changed significantly in this century. We still have lecture formats in most classrooms. We test for minimum competencies, for recall of memorized facts and figures. We organize the school day into periods of 40 to 50 minutes. But how are we organizing students to think, to understand, to grow? By and large, we are still teaching what we have always taught, the way it has usually been taught. Not many schools or teachers have the time, interest, or energy to radically change the way schools work.

What hope is there for the future? Before we get too gloomy about the prospects, let us remember that American schools have done many things extremely well. We have produced a technological leadership that is the envy of the world. Our scientists win Nobel prizes; our economists influence world monetary policy. Our educational system is not a record of failure. It is, by and large, a record of success. The changes that the Information Age requires will come because the changes in society will force the changes in the schools. But that day will not be soon in coming.

In the interim, it is most important that the schools continue to build the careful respect for the quality of human existence on this planet that seems everywhere to be eroding in the pursuit of money and power. Thoreau in *Walden* encouraged his readers to build their "castles in the air. That is where they should be." What we have done today is build some castles in the air, some ideals to dream for, some goals that we can work for, some realities worth achieving. That is where we should be, too. Now, let us put the foundations under them.

DISCUSSION

Professor Lucy Calkins,
Teachers College (English)

I want to thank our speaker for the humanity and warmth of her presentation, and for helping us to end the day with a focus on teachers. Many people have said that the single most important factor in determining the success of a school innovation is the teacher, and his or her role in that intervention.

Certainly the recent work of Cayden, Michaels, and Watson-Gegeo of Harvard University, among others, has shown us that the style and philosophy of a teacher has a lot to do with how that teacher brings computers into the classroom.

For all these reasons, then, it seems crucial that we do everything we can to keep teachers and their needs in the forefront of our thinking. Perhaps, for example, we need to extend Papert's notion of providing a computer for every student so that we also provide a computer for every teacher—for that teacher's personal use. Certainly we need to think about other ways to help teachers feel comfortable being a learner within their school buildings. This point is stressed in the Holmes report:

"As we try to improve teaching and teacher education, then, we cannot avoid trying to improve the profession in which teachers will practice. Here we find a curious situation. While the intellectual and social demands on teachers have escalated at an astonishing rate since the century began, the nature and organization of teachers work have changed only a little since the middle of the 19th Century. Consider these points. Many teachers still instruct whole classes of students in all subjects as there is little or no academic specialization until high school. They still teach classes all day long, with little or no time for preparation analysis or evaluation of their work. They still spend all of their professional time alone with students, leaving little or no time for work with other adult professionals to improve their knowledge or skills, nor are they thought worthy of such endeavors or capable of developing the requisite expertise." The school teacher's job description then is one that none of the universities would ever visit upon a member of their faculty, for universities know that teachers that work under such conditions have no time left to learn, themselves, to be productive scholars or even to do justice to their student's homework. Yet nearly all school teachers hold such creaky old jobs even now in the slick, high tech years of the late 20th century. I guess if we are going to make some of the changes that have been talked about throughout today, I think we need to think about the whole profession of education and the conditions under which our teachers are working.

Professor Bruce Vogeli

I would like to comment specifically on Ms. McGee's concept that there is a dirth of new ideas, a dirth of creative thinking in education. I say that is quite true in education, particularly in the use of technology in education. What I think has happened, and my explanation for why we have not seen a changed attitude toward education in this Information Age is that the window of opportunity for change in education was opened somewhat too soon by the entrepreneurs and innovators in the area of technology. I remember that a decade ago, at our invitation, Patrick Suppes, a graduate of Columbia University, and a personal friend, offered his famous prediction that within a decade all children would have available the same opportunities that Alexander of Macedon had—an electronic tutor, as responsive and knowledgeable as Aristotle. I think that idea simply has not been realized. There has not been an absence of creative thinking, but there has been an absence of the realization of creative ideas. I find now exactly the same situation that Ms. McGee has commented upon, that technology, that computers, have become just another item on the shelf in the media room, just another category of educational technology ancillary to education.

I think that is due to the fact that we simply have not been able to produce the creative software, the carefully crafted software that teachers expected, based upon the promises that were made in the last decade. It is very, very difficult in mathematics to find anything beyond mediocre drill and practice programs that are useful in schools at any grade level. Certainly there are some creative programs, but they are not widely distributed. For the most part, they are not curricularly relevant. The teacher does not see how to use them to advance the objectives of his or her course. I think that the window of opportunity for change in education, resulting from what was predicted a decade ago to be an explosion in software, is almost closed. I think it will be very, very difficult to pry that window open again, especially given the budget restrictions that schools face in this decade and the next. I think we simply promised too much too soon. Teachers, parents, and administrators all over the country were disillusioned by the quality of our software products. It is going to be very tough to get them to reconsider those products and to reopen that window.

We are still making exhorbitant promises—not just in the area of technology, but in all aspects of education. The issue of critical thinking is a good example of the kind of promises that mislead teachers. Publishers all over the country are promising school boards from the California State School Board on down, that their materials will teach critical thinking skills. I think those promises are exhorbitant. They simply cannot be achieved. I think the teaching of critical thinking is not well understood by the greatest teachers alive today. How can we be expected to incorporate in software and in textbooks the extremely subtle processes of problem solving, and of critical thinking.

I would return to my earlier comment that ideas, not technology, should be the focus of educators. Until we have a wealth of ideas with appropriate examples of how these ideas can be implemented in the curriculum, either through traditional texts, creative teaching, or software, we are simply not going to be able to convince our constituents—the parents, the teachers, the administrators who are responsible for American educational programs—to take us seriously.

Professor Judah L. Schwartz,
MIT (Engineering & Education)

There was a man who once said that the cello is an instrument that cannot be played, and the reason he knew that was because he tried it. Maybe some people have not seen software that leads children to make new theorems and to internalize the need for formal proof. But other people have.

It is simply not true that we do not understand. Let me say it differently. I tried very hard to not talk about problem solving, because I find that phrase vacuous. Everything is a problem. Conjugating irregular French verbs is a problem. Solving a differential equation is a problem. Finding TC is a problem. And there's no reason in the world to believe that the solving of any one of them has anything to do with the solving of any other one. So I do not like to talk about problem solving. I like to talk about specific processes. And the issue of inferring the general from the particular is a specific process. The ceremonial catechism of word problems, which is a major piece of the school, which is not tantamount to problem solving, is a specific piece of curriculum. I am not talking about vacuous generalities. I am talking about places in the curriculum and pieces of progress that we have made in understanding human learning and how it can be transmitted in schools, how it can be provoked, implemented, and encouraged in schools. To be sure, I am something of a Pangloss. I have to be something of a Pangloss, otherwise life isn't worth living. But it's not without foundation.

Professor Vogeli.   How many of you know how to teach problem solving?

Professor Schwartz.   I don't, because it's a vacuous phrase.

Professor Vogeli.   How many of you know how to teach heuristics in the teaching of how to solve a simpler problem, or draw a figure, with any degree of reliability, so that student's, say in the seventh or eighth grade, can transfer those skills from one class of problems to another? There must be some math teachers that feel confident that they can teach those kinds of skills.

A (from the audience).   Sure, you were my teacher!

Professor Vogeli.   Touché. I don't know a single math teacher that would guarantee that with a typical student drawn at random from a typical class that those techniques are well enough established in education to guarantee that the students' performance that you are seeking will be attained. I don't believe that we know how to teach those things. I wish I did.

Professor Schwarz.   I would have to answer to that, that it seems to me that we never could guarantee anything before either, nor with the old ways.

Professor Vogeli.   I just finished a review of problem-solving research beginning in 1916 and the clear picture of that research is we don't have any idea of where we're going. It just evolves. It doesn't even spiral, let alone helix. It just sort of wanders. There are people that say that problem-solving research is just about at a level of a breakthrough, that we're realy going to know how students can be taught to attack problems in general—not just word problems.

Beth Lazerick, Computer Education Director, Dalton Schools (graduate of Teachers College)

Some of these gentlemen were my teachers. I am spending this year teaching ninth-grade algebra, second-year algebra class. Every time I get up there I would say, "let's estimate the answer to this problem." One day I took them into the computer lab and we did the problem "Green Globs"—estimating where the lines go through. One child said to me much later, "Miss Lazerick, are you trying to tell us we should try to estimate every time we do everything? You seem to be teaching this to me." I said "thank you," and I walked out of the room. I taught one thing to one child. That's all I can hope to do. I can't teach problem solving. But I can teach a kid to go over and find the Cuisenaire rods to find out what half of 10 is. I can teach a child to go and to draw a picture, or to make a model—not all the time, but sometimes, to estimate, to make a guess. And I think we all do that sometimes. That's all I can hope for. I hope the technology will enable me to have a child say to me, "but I can change that in a word processor." "But I can find it out." And if I can do that, I've won. Teachers College and Judah Schwartz and Kent State University, and the University of Pittsburgh, and 15 years of teaching taught me that. I still look and learn. I'm never going to learn to teach problem solving as well as Pollia. But I'll have to live with that.

General Discussion

Phil Baltzer, RCA Laboratories, Princeton

I just want to reinforce some thoughts that have been expressed here today. We all agree in the inevitable process of technology. The urgency given to us by Professor White is the main thing to consider here. If the educational people do not exercise leadership, the industrial people who see great profit in the educational field will do it, without you, not because they want to do it without you, but because there's not really much leadership in the educational field. What is extremely important is to work toward a partnership with industry that industry will more than be grateful for. Realize that although reflection is necessary, time is of the essence. There really is not a great deal of time for the proverbial chewing of our cud.

Jamie McKenzie, Princeton Schools

I applaud Professor White's question and ask for a comment about collaboration, interdependence, and cooperation in the Information Age as a basic skill.

Leslie Hornig, American Association for the Advancement of Science

Given all the possibilities of technology and the possibilities within technology, how do we make decisions about which ones will be most crucial to teach in the schools? And who is going to make those decisions and what implication does that have for the selection and ultimate implementation of them?

Todd Kelly, Shoreham Wading River School District

There have been two questions addressed from my point of view. One is what curriculum for the Information Age and the other is what technology for the Information Age? We have entered into a new Information Age. As a teacher, I am interested in ideas in how to integrate today's societal demands into my classroom. I can do that through using and attempting to understand the technology myself. For example, I now understand that a word processor has changed my sense of self because I now understand why I never liked the physical act of writing. My mind was always ahead of my hand. I can now share ideas with myself and with others in a way that reveals parts of me that have rarely seen the light of day. Sam Gibbon has attempted to answer the question, What curriculum for the Information Age both today and in his work with "The Voyage of the Mimi" which I've been intimately involved with. He's not the villain of technology come to capture us. If there is a villain of technology, it is us, teachers and teacher educational institutions. If we do not support, encourage, and promote, and even demand the opportunity to interact in both successes and failures, to discover and rediscover what worlds are open to us through interacting with people as well as machines, knowledge as well as information, and data as well as wisdom, then we will be as archaic and dysfunctional as a vacuum tubed Univac.

Hillary Davis, Madison School District

I would like the panelists each to consider the work of Marshall McCluhan in relationship to the language of visual literacy and imagery.

John Pepe, Westport, Connecticut Schools

I guess we have an advantage of historical hindsight in that we have gone through a number of so-called information ages. When Professor White was talking about how to read images I thought to a time before the printing press when the way religious information was conveyed was in the cathedral, with images, and both real and symbolic images. And I thought in a sense that what we're doing is coming back to how we read new kinds of images. The problem that we might be recreating for ourselves is that the kinds of visual images that we had in the middle ages tended to come from a single source and therefore created a monolithic society. The printing press, originally designed to transmit information, had lots of other implications for our political and economic system. I wonder if we go back to the electronic images as a source of information and possibly as a source that's singular, might not we be recreating for ourselves a monolithic situation that we might have gotten rid of 500 or 600 years ago?

Don Richardson, Valhalla High School

Dr. White, I would like you to amplify a very passing reference that I think has great significance to President Reagan and the variety of ways in which he's perceived. I have a very alarming feeling that one following the print media with any scholarly interest, draws one kind of conclusion. On the other hand, one following primarily the television media draws a very different and conflicting and to me personally, very alarming contrast. I wonder if you'd amplify on this phenomenon of our age and what your research says about it.

Catherine Goodan, Nightingale-Banford School

In the last 15 years of my teaching experience I have seen a situation wherein families turn more and more to the schools as a moral educator, the school as an educator in the area of sex, social behavior, you name it. The extended families, the church seem to be less of a factor. As I listened to you I see in sharper focus that there are other sources of information and they are coming indeed through the realm of technology. What concerns me, and what I don't quite know how to deal with, is how are the young going to be able to cope with this information. With this volume? Who is going to control that information? Who's going to select it? Someone a commented about a monolithic product ultimately. I don't know if it's more a question or a reaction.

Michael Snyder, New Jersey Department of Education

This is a personal statement. A couple of years ago I worked on a project that arose out of the Three Mile Island incident. The project was called the Regional Contingency Plan for Education, in case schools would need to be closed down for some reason, Three Mile Island for instance, or for some disease, or whatever. How could schools continue to be educating the children? My project was to develop all kinds of networks—television, newspapers, telephone networks,

U.S. mail, parent–teacher telephone networks, and the like. We designed this program and ran it for 20 days, and pre- and posttested it. We found out that it works. But the teachers did not necessarily like it because they thought that they might be replaced somehow. So we called it a maintenance program, rather than a learning program. One very interesting thing happened. One day we were providing videocassettes for a library. When parents came to see some of the programs, the electricity failed. Everything in the electronic media depends on electricity. It's like putting all your eggs in one basket.

I want to make another point that has to do with how learning. This point is not completely formed in my mind. It has to do with how computers help us to learn about ourselves and how that seems to be a very important part of this new age of learning. What about the Aborigine who stood on one leg and received information from 300 miles away? Or who could anticipate the storms coming and run 50 miles to intercept a storm, to bring water? What about the fire walkers, the people who are now learning through workshops to walk on hot coals? Isn't the human bio-computer the place where we might want to put some of our attention as far as investigation of learning? There are new systems of learning that include accelerated learning processes that have been studied and are indeed being put into action by the Soviets in Bulgaria, and different parts of the world. My last point is that it is not electronic media versus print media, it is fear that will keep us really from learning what we need to learn. For instance, any time a mind-altering substance, whether it be a teacher or some kind of education, whether it be yoga or something new that comes, we have been traditionally afraid because of the radical changes that are possible because of these kinds of things. I just think that culture has to preserve itself through some way. The idea is to have some kind of manageable change, and manageable input.

Janice Rudell, Educational Excellence Network at Teachers College

I wanted to pick up on a couple of points that Professor White made in her chapter. One is the notion of leadership role in education and what that leadership role might be. The other is the very strong entertainment value that so much of the Information Age conveys.

Although I would certainly agree that there is a role for the schools to play in cultivating a kind of media wiseness among students, particularly because the visual imagery of the media is so alluring, so impressionistic. However, given the pervasiveness of the entertainment aspect of the Information Age, and it almost seems to have ushered in a plethora of entertainment, really an epidemic of it, might not there be a leadership role for the schools to play in supporting the values of patience and prolonged study and sustained reflection?

The schools might play a leadership role in examining the extent to which education can become entertainment or should it become entertainment.

RESPONSES

Sam Gibbon

I think the answer to the question about collaboration and cooperation in the Information Age is a useful one. One of the things that can happen once computers are introduced into the classroom, and indeed I think true of the other technologies as well, is that a great deal of social activity and intellectual activity, communal intellectual activity, takes place around the computer, if the software has been designed in that way to encourage that sort of interaction. In my personal view, software that encourages that sort of cooperation and collaboration is superior to software that is intended to engage one student at a time. I think it promotes both peer-teaching and social skills. Both of those seem to be useful.

The question as to who decides on the content, and the treatment the content receives in these new technologies, the answer I think has to be the funding source, whether the funding source is the federal government, the publisher, the state boards of education who in consortia fund technological development, or in the case of commercial television, it be the advertisers and thus, indirectly, consumers. The notion that the technologists can control the content and the treatment that it is given can be over emphasized. The fact of the matter is that the educational administration's use of these technologies in schools has been largely made possible because of the Department of Education and the National Science Foundation over the last 20 years. Without them we would not now be considering the uses of these technologies in education. As that relatively disinterested source of funds disappears, then I think we need to worry about the interested sources of funds that will replace them.

As to the question of the singular monolithic source of images and whether or not we are entering a new middle ages where, in some way, the producer of the image becomes the equivalent of the church, I think the answer is in what will characterize the Information Age, if it doesn't already, that there will be multiple sources of images, and in fact a great diversity of images will be available. This becomes truer as technology becomes cheaper and is delivered into the hands of ordinary folks. It is now possible, in addition to having a half inch videocassette recorder, to have a half inch video camera. It will soon be possible to have a half inch video editing system. There will be the capacity to generate computer graphic images and moving computer graphic images, and computer animation, that is animation assisted by computer. All of these capabilities will be in the home within a matter of a very few years. And then people can be communicating with images in the same way that they presently do, with print, in addition to the ways in which they presently communicate by print. So I think the danger is exaggerated.

Professor Diane Ravitch

There are two or three points I want to respond to.

The first that occurred to me as I was listening to the questions was to wonder whether in searching out where there is a conflict in these chapters, are we talking about the survival of print versus visual images, or are we talking about the survival of the role of the teacher? Are we talking about the survival of the role of the school? I think that although we have skirted the issue to some extent, we may actually be talking about the last of these three because the implications of what Mary Alice White has sketched out really does not imply a school at all. It may imply a total disintegration of the site of learning as we presently know it. The threat, in fact may not be to print literacy, which I see as surviving for a variety of reasons. The threat may be to the schools as we know it. It may turn out to be an archaic institution. There is a certain value to history in that you can look back and say that no matter how many times academics or nostalgic people may have argued for the virtue of the horse over the automobile, it was irrelevant what they argued, because progress has a logic of its own. There are still some people who go riding on horses, but it's for amusement and it's not a means of transportation except for a very, very few people. So that it doesn't really matter whether what we argue is right or wrong, because there's a certain logic to development here which will take over. But I do think that the real threat ultimately may be not to print literacy, but to the school as we presently know it as a place where children gather to be instructed.

Sometimes in these discussions I think that there is a funny kind of nostalgia in which it seems as though there is a longing to revert to pre-Guttenberg days, to the pre-alphabetic eons. Of course the alphabet preceded Guttenberg by thousands of years. He simply developed the first mass printing. But there is a longing to get away from language, as though we would all be somehow more primitive, more spontaneous and more joyful. Then we could read each other's body language rather than have to communicate through written devices. I think as long as we have language, though, and as long as it is reduced to words, there's a tremendous value to this. I think that we human beings do have a limited Rom capacity, and so I to have some notes that I'm referring to because of my limited Rom.

What I am arguing here is that we need balance. We need to have both the tremendous insight that Professor White has brought to the discussion, the

sense of urgency that we cannot continue to operate a horse and buggy opera-
tion and turn our back on these new technologies. But at the same time, we
need to recognize that there are things that even the best of the new technology
cannot yet do and may possibly never be **able** to do.

I think about an argument one often hears in education, and I have seen it
made over the decades, and that is "Well, man, this is where it's happening, let's
go with the flow." This is the new thing and you've got to be with it—if you are
not on top of this trend you're going to be left behind. It's led to a tremendous
amount of trendiness in education. There are, I might remind us, lots of things
that are happening that we don't want to go with. There is a lot of child abuse.
But we do not teach child abuse in the schools. We teach children to be wary of
child abusers. We know there is a lot of drug abuse, that it has been a spreading
disease in our society and other modern industrial societies. We do not teach
children which drugs to smoke and how to smoke them wisely. We try to urge
them not to use them. There is a lot of rape. There is a lot of murder. There is a
lot of terrible things that go on. But the fact that they are happening, they are
spreading, and they seem to be endemic to our kind of modern industrial world,
does not mean that we have to learn to live with them. We still try in our
schools to develop curricula to try to prevent them from happening. In other
words, we try to make in the schools a counterbalance to what we see as
negative social forces that means that we try to use their intelligence to
discriminate between what we want to encourage, what we want to wisely
defend and protect, and what we want to advocate. So my plea, as it was in my
chapter, is to be neither for, nor against, print literacy or technology, but rather
to understand that these are both part of the learning devices, learning tools
that are powerful and not to ignore the power of either of them.

Professor Mary Alice White

I'll respond only to the suggestion that I talk about the present Reagan
administration's use of imagery, which I will do extremely briefly. I think the best
argument I could make for teaching children how to read images is this
administration's use of images.

Index

art, 12–14

basic skills, Information Age, 61–62
Bateson, G., 18
Bower, G., 44, *66*

Calkins, L., 73–74, 88–89
compact disc, 16
computers, 28
CPB, vii
Cuban, L., 27, *39*
curriculum, 1–99

data bases, 16
databases, 70
decision making, 85–87
Department of Communications, vii
Dewey, J., 19, 21, 37

Edison, T., 27
educators, education of, 68–69
Electronic Learning Laboratory, vii, viii
Ellul, J., 25, *39*
epistemology, 18
estimating, 92
evaluating quality of information, 61, 82–84

Forster, E. M., 26

Gibbon, S., 1–24, 97–98
Gross, R., 27, *39*

Hawkins, 22
Hertzberg, H., 19–21, 36–38, 63–65
Hutchins, R., 34, *39*

imagery comprehension, 62–63
imagery, effect on human behavior, 54–56
inequity, in technologies, 71
information, 3
Information Age, 2–99
information, shaping of, 47–50
ITTE, vii

Jacobson, W., 21–23, 38–39, 65

Kosslyn, S., 44, *66*

Landsat, 2
language, 68
leadership, educational, 93, 96
locus of memory, 46–47